ISBN 978-1-332-03712-4
PIBN 10273747

English
Français
Deutsche
Italiano
Español
Português

www.forgottenbooks.com

Mythology Photography **Fiction**
Fishing Christianity **Art** Cooking
Essays Buddhism Freemasonry
Medicine **Biology** Music **Ancient
Egypt** Evolution Carpentry Physics
Dance Geology **Mathematics** Fitness
Shakespeare **Folklore** Yoga Marketing
Confidence Immortality Biographies
Poetry **Psychology** Witchcraft
Electronics Chemistry History **Law**
Accounting **Philosophy** Anthropology
Alchemy Drama Quantum Mechanics
Atheism Sexual Health **Ancient History**
Entrepreneurship Languages Sport
Paleontology Needlework Islam
Metaphysics Investment Archaeology
Parenting Statistics Criminology
Motivational

TREVELYAN PAPERS.

PART II.

A.D. 1446 — 1643.

EDITED BY

J. PAYNE COLLIER, ESQ.

PRINTED FOR THE CAMDEN SOCIETY.

M.DCCC.LXIII.

WESTMINSTER :
PRINTED BY JOHN BOWYER NICHOLS AND SONS.
25, PARLIAMENT STREET.

[NO. LXXXIV.]

CONTENTS.

NOTICE.

In addition to the documents contained in this and in the previous Part of "The Trevelyan Papers," the Council has had placed in its hands a large mass of family correspondence, principally of the seventeenth century, together with numerous charters; relating, for the most part, to families and estates in the Western Counties, and of much interest to the topographer or local antiquary: of the charters a considerable number has been presented by Sir W. C. Trevelyan to the British Museum, for better preservation, and easier access. Whether any, or what portion of these, it may be expedient hereafter to print, must depend mainly upon the funds the Council may have at its disposal for such a purpose.

TREVELYAN PAPERS.

SIR WILLIAM CAVENDISH'S BOOK.ª

THE BOKE OF THE COPIES OF THE CERTYFICAT MADE TO THE KINGES Mᴬᵗᵉˢ COUNSELL.

The Clerke of the Hamper (MˡMˡ li); the receyvor of the Duchey A.D. 15 of Lancaster (iiijᵐˡ li); and lackinge this yere of the Duchey of Cornewall (Mˡ Mˡ li) * * * the office of the receyver of Wardes Landes (iiijᵐ li) and lyveries; and likewise lackinge this yere of the revenues of the merques of Exitors (M merks) landes, with many other thinges insident to the forsaid Office, amountinge yerely in the hole to xiiijᵐ li or there abowtes, now taken of them by warrauntes directyd from the Kinges Maᵗᵗᵉ and his honorable counsaill, as more at large shall apere in a boke almoste made by the Surveyors, declaring the hole intere office of generall Survey, which prevencion of receiptes hathe and clerely shall disorder the same Office, bringinge ordenary Receiptes furre owte of their righte course, whiche (as it is said) hathe byn the chefest releaff of the furniture of the same Thesaurer; and withoute the same thinges

---

ª The latest marginal date in Part I. of "The Trevelyan Papers" is 1551, when the Earl of Southampton made his will, of which we gave a copy (p. 206). We now turn back for a few years, viz., to 1545.6, for the purpose of inserting some valuable particulars from the original book of Sir William Cavendish, who at that date filled the important office of Treasurer of the Chamber to Henry VIII. It is a small folio in a vellum wrapper; and, although apparently kept by a clerk, much of it, including various corrections, is in the hand-writing of Sir William. A very small portion, denoted here by asterisks, has been damaged by damp, and is therefore not legible.

reduced into the olde order and trade, shall not be able to paye any foreyn Warrauntes or Depechis, but onely the bare ordenarye. Therfore it is very necessarye and mete to consider the state of this Office.

Money receyved by William Cavendishe, Esquier, Thesaurer to the Kinges Highnes of his most honorable Chamber, from the xixth daye of February Anno xxxvij^{mo}, untill the xx daye of Marche then next followinge.ᵃ

Firste of Lewys ap Watkyn for Londes in Karmarden
    shere .   .   .   .   .   .   cj^{li} xvj^s viij^d ob. q^r.
Of Thomas Streniholde for atteinted Landes in
    Yorkeshere .   .   .   .   .   .   xxxix^{ll} xij^s iiij^d
Of Thomas Hall for atteynted Landes in Lincoln shere   liiij^{ll} x^s v^d
Of Henry Bradshawe, Esqr for his Tenthes .   .   xiij^s x^d ob.
Of John Kychen for the atteynted landes in Whalley   clvj^{ll} v^s vj^d
Of Richard Worseley, Esquier, for Landes in the Isle
    of Wighte .   .   .   .   .   .   iiij^{xx}ij^{li} xv^s iiij^d
Of Sir Rauff Sadler, Knighte, hie Treasorer of the
    Kinges Ma^{tes} Warres ageynste Scotlande, upon
    the determination of his Accompte   clxiij^{ll} xvj^s x^d ob.
Of Thomas Joens, knight, for the atteynted Landes
    of Sr Rice Griffithe .   .   .   .   cviij^d vij^s vj^d
Of Will'm Pynnocke for Warwicke and Spencer's Landes   cxx^{ll}
Of Lewice Joens, Shreff, Brekenockes in Wales   xij^{li} xij^s iiij^d
Of Michell Wentworthe, Esquier, for the Landes
    late the Duke of Clarence   .   .   lxj^{ll} xvj^s viij^d ob.

ᵃ That is to say, from Feb. 1545, to March 1546. This book, with the detailed accounts of receipts and payments, establishes Sir W. Cavendish's statement respecting the disorganisation of the office of Treasurer of the Royal Chamber. The particulars are nearly all of considerable interest, not merely from the historical names introduced into the accounts, but from the public information to be gleaned from them.

Of Olyver Franckelyn for atteynted Landes of the
    Countis of Salisbury .   .   .   .   . cc^{li}

Of Sir Thomas Arrundell, Knight, for the Dukdum of Cornewall $M^{l\ li}$

Of the same Sir Thomas Arrundell, Knighte, for the
    same Dukedum .   .   .   .   . $viij^{li}$

Of James Morrice, Esquier, for Richemondes Landes $ccclxviij^{li}$

Of Sir John Horselye, Knighte, for Huntingdon
    Landes .   .   .   .   .   . $cxix^{li}\ xij^{s}\ v^{d}$

Of Thomas Arrundell, Knight, for the Dukedum of Cornewall $iiij^{c\ li}$

Of Sir John Will'ms, knight, for Buckingham
    Landes .   .   .   .   . $lxxij^{li}\ vj^{s}\ j^{d}$ ob. di.

Of John Savage, Esquier, for recovered Landes $lxvj^{li}\ xiij^{s}\ iiij^{d}$

Of Edward Tyndall for Barkleis Landes $ccxj^{li}\ xvj^{s}\ viij^{d}$

Of Sir George Herbert, Knighte, for landes in Glamorganshere c^{li}

Of Thomas Spurwaye for atteynted landes of the lorde
    marques of Exitor   . $ix^{c}iij^{li}\ xj^{s}\ xj^{d}$ ob. di. ij ps ob.

Of Edmonde Pecham, Knight, for Landes in Aldeforde c^{li}

Of Richard Grenwaye, Esquier, for landes late quene Jane's $ccxix^{li}$

Of Sir Rice Maxewell, Knighte, chamberlein of Chester $iiij^{xx}xix^{li}\ x^{d}$

Of Robert Henege, Esq., M^{r} of the Woodsales $ciiij^{xx}xj^{li}\ x^{s}\ x^{d}$

Of Sir Thomas Seymer, Knighte, for londes in
    Bromefelde .   .   .   .   .   . $ccxix^{li}\ v^{s}\ iiij^{d}$

Of Will'm Pynnocke for Warwickes landes $xlvij^{li}\ x^{s}\ v^{d}\ q^{r}$

Of the same Will'm Pinnocke for the same
    landes .   .   .   .   . $cccxliiij^{li}\ xiiij^{s}$ ob. q^{r}.

Of Sir George Herbert, Knighte, for landes in Gla-
    morgein shere .   .   .   .   . $liiij^{li}\ ij^{s}\ iij^{d}$ ob. q^{r}.

Of James Morrice for Richemonde landes . $ccclij^{li}\ xv^{s}\ ix^{d}$ ob.

Of Thomas Spurwey for the marques of Exitor's landes $xlvj^{li}$

Of Robert Gryffyth for landes in Ruthin .   . $xx^{li}\ xj^{s}\ vij^{d}$

Of Sir Thomas Seymer, Knighte, for landes in
    Cherkerlande .   .   .   .   .   . $xxiiij^{li}\ ij^{s}\ x^{d}$

Of John Ryther, Esquier, for the atteinted Landes of
    Thomas Crumwell late Erle of Essex $clxxiij^{li}\ xij^{s}\ viij^{d}$

Of Will'm Morrice for atteynted landes of the Lorde
    Hungerforde   .   .   .   .   .   .   iiij^{xx} ^{li}

Of Anthony Harvy, Esquier, for the atteinted Landes
    of the Marques of Exitor   xxxv^{li} xvij^s v^d ob.

Of the same Anthony Harvye for the same landes   xxxj^{li} ij^s xj^d q^r.

Of Will'm Pinnocke, Esquier, for Coparsioners Landes   xxxvj^{li} xij^d

Of Anthony Knevet for landes in Denbigh   vij^{li} xj^s ij^d ob.

Of William Gery for landes late William Howardes   xx^{li}

Of Sir Richerd Buckeley, Knighte, Chamberlein of
    Northwales   .   .   .   .   .   v^{li} ix^s viij^d

Of George Rawley for the atteinted landes of James
    Fitzgarret   .   .   .   .   .   xxxiij^{li} xvij^s iiij^d

Of John Holcrofte, Esquier, for atteynted Landes of
    the Pryory of Lynton   .   .   .   .   xlv^{li} xix^s xj^d

Of the Lorde Ferrys for Landes in West Haverforde lviij^{li} xviij^s v^d ob.

Of Thomas Arrundell, Knighte, for the Dukedum of
    Cornewall   .   .   .   .   .   cccxlvij^{li} xj^s j^d ob.

Of Will'm Morrice for the atteinted Landes of the
    Lorde Hungerforde   xliij^{li} xiij^s xj^d

Of Sir Edward Crofte, knight, rec. in Wales   .   ccliij^{li} ix^s iiij^d

Of Lorde Henry Erle of Worcetor for Landes in
    Monnegomery   .   .   .   .   vij^{li} xj^s v^d ob. q^r. di.

Of Roger Amyce for Landes in Glaston and Redinge xj^{li} vij^s viij^d di q^r.

Of the Lorde Ferris for Londes in the Countie of Pembr. cvij^{li} xv^s

Of John Pakington, Esquier, upon determination of
    . his Accompte   .   .   .   .   .   ix^{li} vj^s iiij^d

Of the Lord Ferris chamberlein of Southwales   xj^{li} xixd

Of Rice up Guill'm   .   .   .   .   .   xxiij^{li} ij^s

Of John Markeham, Knighte, for the landes of
    Jasper Dukke of Bed.*   .   .   .   xxxj^{li} x^s ij^d

Of Thomas More for landes in Medenham   ix^{li} ij^s iiij^d

---

* Sic in *MS*, and probably intended for Jasper Duke of Bedford, who died without issue in 1495, when the title became extinct.

Obligacions.

Of Nicholas Poyens and Will'm Vaughan   c markes

Of John Grenehill   .   ..   .   xx^{li}

Of Will'm Brereton   .   .   .   .   .   xiij^{li} vj^s viij^d

Of Lorde Fraunces Erle of Shrewisbury   cc^{li}

Of Roger Woodhouse, Esquier   xxxiij^{li} vj^s viij^d

Of Richerd Tycheborne   .   .   .   .   .   c^{li}

Of Michell Haywarde   .   .   .   .   vj^{li} xiij^s iiij^d

Summa totalis of all the Receites   vij^{ml}DCCCiiij^{xx}xvj^{li} iiij^s iij^d di. q^r.

Wherof paid.

To Mr Anthonye Auger, John Myners, and Jerrerd
     Goore by the Kinges councelles letters   M$^{l\ li}$

To the Comyssioners of the marches of Wales   DDxviij^{li} xviij^s xi^d

To Sir Richerd Lee, Knighte, Surveyor of the Kingis
     workes within his grace's realme   D^{li}

To Sir Edwarde Kerne, Knighte, Ambassadour in
     Flaunders   .   .   .   .   .   .   CCxxxvj^{li}

To Edmonde Harvell, the Kinges Ambassador in Venice   cc^{li}

To the Lady Anne of Cleves   xxxvj^{li} xiij^s iiij^d

To William Ibgrave, the Kinges enbroder   ciiij^{xx}xiiij^{li} xiij^s x^d

To Spendley, the golde drawer   .   .   cclviij^{li} ij ^{s} iiij^d

To Pero Doulxe, the Frenshe Coke .   .   x^{li}

To the M^r of the postes .   ..   .   .   .   iiij$^{c\ li}$

To my Clerke of the Courte for payment of wages
     withe messengers billes and other depeches in
     the courte   .   .   .   .   M$^{l\ li}$

Paid upon quarter dayes and half yeres for parte due
     in Sr Bryan Tuke's tyme and Sr Anthony Rous
     tyme *   .   .   .   .   .   .   M^{l}CCCxxij^{li} xviij^s x^d

Summa totalis of all the paymentes   v^{m}CCClxxvij^{li} viij^s iiij^d

And so remaynethe   .   .   .   .   M^{l}M^{l}Dxviij^{li} xvj^s di q^r.

---

* Sir Brian Tuke was Treasurer of the King's Chamber in 1529 (See Trevelyan Papers,
Part I. p. 36). Sir Anthony Rous had also filled the same office before Sir W. Cavendish
was placed in it.

Memorand.—There is to be paid in in money due before my entre into the said office, as apereth by a boke made of the partyculers thereof signed with thandes of the Surveyors   M^lDCCCxlviij^{li} xviij^s xj^d

---

Money due at this our Lady daye for wages and other charges to be paid by the Thesaurer of the Kinges Chamber.

Firste for quarter's wages and halff yeres wages due at this our present Lady daye	M^lM^{l li}
To my Clerke at the Courte for monthes wages with messengers billes, and depeches, in the courte, after the rate of iiij^{c li} a moneth, for the moneth of Marche	CCCC^{li}
To the M^r of the Postes due at this present . .	DCC^{li}
To the Commyssioners of the Marches of Wales for our Lady daye	CCxviij^{li} xviij^s xj^d
To Sr Richerd Lee, Knighte, for Feb. and Marche	CC^{li}
To Mr. Kerne, the Kinges Ambassador in Flaunders	clxviij^{li}
To Edward Harvell, the Kinges Ambassador in Venice	c^{li}
To the Lady Anne Cleves	xxxvj^{li} xiij iiij^d
To Edward Courteney for his diettes at iiij^{li} a moneth	xij^{li}
To the Kinges Almenor upon good friday . .	c^{li}
To the Kinges goldesmythe upon his grace's warrauntes	M^lv^{li} x^s ij^d
To Mr. Vaughan, Captain of Portesmouth for iij monethes nowe due	CClxxvij^{li} vj^s v^d
Summa totalis to be paid at our Lady Daye	v^m CCxviij^{li} vj^s v^d

Money due to be paid for Midsomer quarter Anno xxxvij°

For quarter's wages due at Midsomer . . .	M^lD^{li}
To my Clerke of the Courte. &c. by reason of this warre tyme	M^lCC^{li}
To the M^r of the Postes for Aprill, Maye, and June, by estimation, by reason of this warre, at ij^{c li} a moneth	DC^{li}
To the Comyssioners of the Marches of Wales	CCxviij^{li} xviij^s xj^d

To Sr Richerd Lee, Knighte, Surveyor of the Kinges
workes, for Aprill, May, and June by the Ks. war-
raunt dormaunt, after the rate of c^{li} a moneth   ccc^{li}

To Mr. Kerne, &c. . . . .   clxviij^{li}

To Edmonde Harvell, &c. . . . . . .   c^{li}

To Mr. Vaughan, Capt., of Portesmouth   cclxxvij^{li} iiij^s

To Edward Courteney for iij monthes. . . .   xij^{li}

To the Lady Anne Cleves . . . . . xxxvj^{li} xiij^s iiij^d

Summa totalis to be paid at Midsomer   iiij^mccccxij^{li} xvj^s iij^d

Money due to be paid at Michelmas quarter, Anno xxxviij°.

For quarter wages and halff yeres wages . .   M^lM^{l li}

To my clerke, &c. by reason of this warre tyme, by
estymation at iiij^{c li} a month . . . .   M^lcc^{li}

To the M^r of the Postes, &c. . . . .   Dc^{li}

To the Commyssioners of the Marches of Wales   ccxviij^{li} xviij^s xj^d

To Sir Richerd Lee, Knt., Surveyor, &c. . . .   ccc^{li}

To Mr. Kerne, &c. . . . . . .   clxviij^{li}

To Edmonde Harvell, &c. . . . . . .   c^{li}

To Mr. Vaughan, Captaigne of Portesmouth   cclxxvij^{li} iiij^s

To the Lady Anne of Cleves .   xxxvj^{li} xiij^s iiij^d

To Edward Courteney for iij monthes . . .   xij^{li}

Summa totalis to be paid at Mighelmas   iiij^mDccccxiJ^{li} xvj^s iij^d

---

The Copie of a brieff Estimate and vewe and declaracion made
of the Kinges Ma^{tes} Dettes, desperat dettes, and sperat
dettes, and dettes, (sic) and whiche be sperat dettes, and not
due, as followeth: to the Kinges maiestie and his Councell.

A brefe estimate, viewe, and declaracion of the presente state of
the Kinges debtes, made and gathered oute of Sir Brian Tuke's bokes
by Sir Will'm Cavendishe, now Thesaurer of the Kinges Chamber,
growen upon obligacions, Tailles, and other spocialties, aswell in
the tyme of the Kinge of famous memory, Henry the vijth, as in

the Kinge our sovereigne lordes tyme that nowe is, remayninge in the Treasory of the same Office in the charge and kepinge of the executors of the said Sir Brian Tuke, not as yet delyvered; and for because the said Sir Will'm Cavendishe, nowe Treasorer, is in this rome a yonge Officer not longe exercised in the same, and the bokes of the said Sir Brian Tuke interlaced, intricked, and in many places dowtfull and uncerteigne howe he maye truely and justely take them,[*] hathe compyled this matter as a viewe and breff declaracion wherby his Majestie may neverthelesse perceyve what a charge and burden the said Treasorer shall shortely receyve of specialties, obligacions, and tailles, many of them not semyng worthy kepinge as he supposeth, and yet of as greate charge and burden as the beste leviable dettes. And also, for because many of the said obligacions and specialties, beynge entred in the boke of obligations with a visage of a greate debte, semeth by him upon the perusinge and examynacion of the same bokes to be of litle or none effect, The humble peticion and requeste of the seid Sir Will'm Cavendishe is that, upon consideracions hereafter followinge (yf it shall seme good to the Kinges moste excelent Maiestie), Commissioners, eyther of his highnes moste honorable Councell, or any other whome his grace shall please to name, may peruse, examyn, and trye, whiche be sperat and good debtes, and which been mere desperat and will never revyve, before the seid Treasorer shalbe charged and burdened with the receit of the said Obligacions, Tailles, or other specialties, so that aswell the said Treasorer, as all the Courte of Surveyors, knowinge the pleasuer of his highnes herein, may, upon reporte made to his Maiestie therof, procede further as to their moste bounden duties shall apperteigne. The grose or totall, bothe good sperat and desperat, conteyned in the said Sir Bryan Tuke's boke here apereth, amounting to the somme of cccxxij^{mi}ix^{c}iiij^{xx}ij xiijs x^{d}.

---

* Hence it appears that Sir Bryan Tuke (only Bryan Tuke *Esquire* in 1529) had left the accounts of his office in great confusion, and that various necessary documents for clearing up the doubts that had arisen were still in the hands of the previous Treasurer's executors.

.t is to saye: upon

igacions yet remaynynge for the performaunce of
Covenauntes and other Condicions, aswel in the
tyme of Kinge Henry the viij^th, as also in the tyme
of the Kinges Matei that nowe is   lxix^mlDiiij^xxj^li xix^s iij^d
ers Tailles yet remaynynge   .   viij^mlCCCClxxix^li x^s vij^d
igacions yet remaynynge in. the tymes of Kinge
Henry the viij^th and the Kinges Matie that nowe
is, dowtefull whether they be good or de-
sperate   .   .   .   .   ciiij^xxxiiij^mDCCix^li vij^s ix^d
igacions of diverse parsons whose dettes be supposed to be good and due   xxviij^mlDxxxiiij^li x^s j^d
er obligacions there be for the debtes of divers
parsons thought good and not yett due   xxj^mDClxxv ^li vj^s ij^d

---

Money paid sins the xxviijth day of Januar. abovseide, that is,
from the deathe of our late sovereigne Lorde^a untill the
xxth day of Marche in the firste yere of the reigne of our
sovereigne Lorde Kinge Edwarde the sixt, that nowe is.

ney p'd to Thempror's and Frenche K's Embassador by wey of Rewarde   .   .   .   .   .   CCCC^li.
Sir Raulfe Sadler, M^r of the Wardrobe, for part
of the K's Creditors that dede is,   .   MDCxxxiiij^li vj^s viij^d
Rob'te Legge, Tresorer of the shippes,   M^li.
In the hole   .   .   .   .   .   iij^mlxxxiiij^li vj^s viij^d
the margin.   By Bill signed by my Lord Protector's Grace
hand and the Counsell MMxxxiiij^livj^s viij^d; Wherof, by bill
signed by Counselles' handes allonly   M^li
ney p'd for charges at the courte monethly as
aboveseide   .   .   .   iiij^clxxij^li iij^s v^d

To Sir Raulfe Sadler, M^r of the Wardrobe, for part
of the K's Creditors that dede is,   .   MDCxxxiij^{ll} vj^s viij^d

To Rob'te Legge, Tresorer of the shippes,   M^{ll}.

In the hole   .   .   .   .   .   iij^{ml}xxxiij^{ll} vj^s viij^d

In the margin.   By Bill signed by my Lord Protector's Grace
hand and the Counsell MMxxxiij^{ll}vj^s viij^d; Wherof, by bill
signed by Counselles' handes allonly   M^{ll}

Money p'd for charges at the courte monethly as
aboveseide   .   .   .   .   iiij^clxxij^{ll}iiij^s v^d

^a Henry VIII. having died 28 Jan. 1547, Sir W. Cavendish was continued in his
office by Edward VI.

Money p'de to therle of Sussex at the K's grace's Coronacon   xx^s
To the Surveior of the K's workes   .   .   .   cc^{ll}
To the M^r of the Poostes   .   .   .   ix^{c}lxviij^{ll} iiij^s
Summe of the p^{tes} from the xxviijth day of Jan^{ry},
     being the daye of the Kg's dethe, untill the xxth
     day of M^{che} A^o primo R^e E. vj^{ti} iiij^{ml}DCiiij^{xx}xiij^{ll} xiiij^s j^d

----

The totall Summ of all the paymentes within thoffice of the
said Treasorer.

Summe of all the paymentes made by Sir Will'm
     Cavendishe, Knight, Treasaurer of the Kinges
     Chamber for one hole yere, ended the last daie
     of Marche Anno primo R.R. Edw^l vj^{ti} xxxvj^{ml}CCCxx^{ll} x^s xj^d q.

The office of the Treasorer of the Kinges Chamber.

Paymentes made by my Clerke at the Courte   viij^{m}DCCxxxv^{ll} vij^d q.
Quarter's wages, half-yeres wages, and other ordynary
     paymentes made by my Clerkes at London xix^{ml}CCCClvj^{ll} ix^s xj^d
Extraordynary paymentes, aswell by the Kinges
     warrauntes as the Kinges Counsailles Letters   viij^{ml}Cxxix^{ll} v^d
There is commen in by warrauntes to be paied yerely
     by annuities within thoffice abovesaied sins the
     deathe of our late sovereigne Lorde King Henry
     theight   .   .   .   .   .   .   DCCCiiij^{ll} ix^s iiij^d
To the Clerke of the stable by the K's warraunt
     cccx^{ll}. To Grafton the K's printer by warr. CCviij^{ll}.
     To the Armorers for their cootes, gownes, and
     hoscine lxij^{ll}. In thole   .   .   .   .   .   Diiij^{xx} ^{ll}

A Declaracion made by the Treasorer of the Kinges Chamber, aunswering to the contents of the bill to him directed from Sir Will'm Paget, Knight, one of the Kinges most honorable Counsaill, and Sir Walter. Mildemaye, Knight, one of the generall Receyvors of the Kinges Landes, dated the xxixth day of December, 1548.

To the firste.[a] There remayneth in the said office in redy mony the said xxixth daye of December above wrytten nothing. The Office being indebted to dyvers and sondry persons in the somme of xiiij^m ^{li}, or therabout, as appereth by dyvers Certificates heretofore made unto the Kinges most honorable Counsaill, as by the same redy to be shewed playnlye appereth at large.

To the seconde. There remayneth in the said office one warraunt for the Clerke of the Kinges stable not yet fully paid by the somme of cvij^{li} xiiij^s xj^d. Neverthelesse there hathe been brought and shewed within the same office by dyvers persons many warrauntes not receyved for want of monye to aunswer the same.

To the thirde. There bathe been receyved yerely into the said office by two yeres passed, and afore that tyme, of Revenues, Pynes, and other casualties aforesaid into the said office syns the last daye of Marche last past, but onely iiij^{m}DCCxxxvij^{li} xij^s viij^d, wherof receyved Of the receyvor of the dukedom of Lancaster MMiiij^{c}l ^{li}. Of the receyvor of Wardes and Lyveries M^{li}, and upon Obligacions M^{l}CCiiij^{xx}vij^{li} xij^s viij^d.

To the fourth. I cannot certainlye as yet aunswere what the total somme amounteth unto of all the specyalties and bandes which shoulde remayne in my office and charge, for that I have not receyved them all, beyng but nowe on receyving parte of theym by the executors of Sir Bryan Tuke and the Awditors; and therfore for a perfit declaracion of this Article it were mete to call the

---

[a] i. e. " to the first " interrogatory or question propounded by Sir William Paget and Sir Walter Mildmay, who had been specially appointed to inquire into the state of the office of Treasurer of the Kiug's Chamber.

Awditors that have perused and made bokes of all the same specialties, and of theym you may knowe the truth. Notwithstonding by a boke remanyng in my office collected by Sr Thomas Moyle and Sr Walter Mildmay, Knightes, and the Awditors, supposed sperate and good, and due at this present day, amounteth to the somme of xxviij^{m}ix^{c}iiij^{xx}xj ^{li} xiiij^s xi^d ob. q.

To the fyfte.   There is yerely paid in fees, wages, annuyties, and other ordynary paymentes, whiche must contynewe, the somme of xxv^{m}cc^{li}, wherof paid monthly DC^{li}, quarterly MMMD^{li}, and half yerely MM^{li}; wherof in fees duringe lief, having there begynnyng in the tyme of the said S^r W'm Cavendishe, amounteth to the somme of iiij^{c}lj ^{li} xviij^s vj^d. And in fees during pleasure, having there begynnyng in lyke maner in the tyme of the said Sir Will'm Cavendishe, amounteth to the somme of MCCCiiij^{xx}xix ^{li} ij^s.   And xxiij^{m}cccxlviij ^{li} xix^s vj^d in other fees and annuyties not knowen to the said Sr Will'm Cavendishe whether thei be during pleasure or lief, whiche fees some had there begynnyng and were paid afore in the tyme of Sr Thomas Wyat,[a] Sir Brian Tuke, and Sr Anthony Rous, late Treasorers there.   The patentes for the whiche remayne not in the said office.   But for discharge of payment of the said sommes to theim by the said Sr Will'm Cavendishe in lyke manner as there was before his tyme, there remayneth in the said office a warraunt signed with thand of our late sovereigne Lorde King Henry theight. Also ther is paid to Ambassadours, the Comyssioners of the Marches of Wales, and other that must cease, MM^{li}.

---

[a] Hence we learn that Sir Thomas Wyatt, the poet, had filled the office of Treasurer before Sir Brian Tuke and Sir Anthony Rous. That Sir Henry Wyatt had been so is known.

The Kinges booke of Receyptes and Paymentes Receyved A.D. 15 and Payed by [Sir] Willi[am] Cavendyshe, knight, Tresaurer of the Kynges Majesties Chamber, begynninge the Fyrste daye of October Anno regni Regis Edwardi Sexti secundo, and endyng the laste daie of Septembre anno Regni Regis Edwardi Sexti predicti Tercio, being one hole yere.*

[The receipts are stated monthly, and they amount in the whole to the sum of 16,868*l.* 12*s.* the total being thus introduced : *Sum'a omnium Receptionum, ab ultimo die Septembris Anno regni Regis Edwardi Sexti Secundo, usque ad primam diem Octobris, Anno Tercio regni Regis Edwardi sexti predict', vis. per spacium unius Anni integri.* The payments are thus headed :]

Paymentes made by Sir William Cavendyshe, knight, Treasourer of the Kinges Majesties Chamber, from the laste daye of September in the Seconde yere of the reigne of our sovereigne lorde King Edwarde the Sixte, untill the firste daye of October in the thirde yere of the Reigne of our saied Sovereigne Lorde Kinge Edwarde the Sixte.

Ordynary Paymentes made in October Anno regni Regis Edwardi Sexti Secundo.

Sondaye at Otelandes.

Fyrste for the Kinges offeringe this Sondaye:
Item for the Kinges daily Almese this weeke
                                     Nil quia non sol. hoc mens.

Sondaye at Otelandes.

Item for the Kinges offeringe this Sonday
Item for the Kinges daily Almese this weeke
                 } nil ca^a pred'a.

Sondaye at Otelandes.

Item for the Kinges offeringe this Sondaye
Item for the Kinges offeringe on Saint Lukes daye } nil ca^a ut supra.
Item for the Kinges daily Almese this weeke

* The original volume from which the following extracts are made is similar to that extracted from and described in Trevelyan Papers, Part i. p. 191. Both volumes are described in the preface to Nichols's Literary Remains of Edward VI. p. xx *g.* They have been presented by Sir W. C. Trevelyan to the Record Office.

Sondaye at Otelandes.

Item for the Kinges offeringe this Sondaye
Item for the Kinges offeringe on Symon and Judes } nil ca⁸ ut supra.
    day . . . .

Item for the Kinges daily Almese this weeke .   xxxvij⁵ xj^d

Item to Hughe Lee, clerke of tharmorye at Grene-
    wiche, for the wages of the Almaigne Armorers
    there for one monethe, &c. .   xxviij^li xvj⁵ ix^d

Item paied to Frauncis Evered, gent. Usher of the
    Kinges Ma^tes Chamber, for him selfe and yoman
    Usher, foure yomen and fower Gromes, for
    makinge ready the Kinges Lodginges at Ote-
    landes by the space of two daies. And also for
    makinge ready the quenes syde for the lord
    protectour his grace, as appereth by a bill signed
    by the Lorde Chamberlaine his hande, the some of   xl⁵

Item paied to Sir John Markham, knight, lieutenaunte
    of the Kinges Ma^tes Tower of London, for the
    dyettes and other necessaries of Edwarde Cour-
    teneye for viij monethes &c. .   xliiij^li iiij⁵

Monethes wages in October.

Item to Philip van Welder, Luter	xlvj⁵ viij^d
Item to Peter van Welder, Luter	xxxj⁵
Item to William Moore, harper	xxxj⁵
Item to Thomas Kent, singingeman . . .	xxv⁵ vj^d
Item to Thomas Bowde, singingeman . . .	xxv⁵ vj^d
Item to Richarde Woodwarde, plaier on the bagpipe	xx⁵ viij^d
Item to Nicholas Puvall, mynstrell . . .	xlj⁵ iiij^d
Item to Hughe Pallard, mynstrell . . .	xxxj⁵
Item to Edwarde Lacke, mynstrell . . .	xxxj⁵
Item to Thomas Alye, mynstrell . . .	xxxj^i
Item to Thomas Curzon, mynstrell . . .	xxxj⁵

Item to Robert Maye, mynstrell   .   xxxj^s
Item to Alaine Robson, mynstrell   .   xxxj^s
Item to Thomas Pagington, mynstrell   xxxj^s
Item to the Children of the Kinges majesties Chappell
    for their bourde wages   .   .   .   .   .   xxvj^s viij^d
Item to Richerde Cycell, yoman of the Kinges robes   xxx^s
Item to Clement Harleston, oystringer   .   .   .   xxxj^s
Item to the Gromes of the Buckhounds for fynding
    of the Kinges buckhounds meate   .   .   .   xxij^s ij^d
Item to Richard Catteline, keeper of the Kinges pondes   xv^s vj^d
Item to Sir John Wulfe, preist, maker and deviser of
    the Kinges herbors and plantes of grafts   .   .   xx^s viij^d
Item paied to Sir Thomas Darcey, knight, Master of
    the Kinges majesties Armory at Grenewich, for
    gownes, dublettes, and hoseine for twentie foure
    Armorers, &c.   .   .   .   .   .   .   xxx^{li}

Ordynary Paymentes in November, 2 *Edw. VI.*

Sondaye at Hamptoncourte.

Item for the Kinges offering this Sondaye
Item for the Kinges offering at Masse of the holy ⎱ nil dicta causa.
    ghooste, the furst daye of the Parliament ⎰
Item paied to Phelip Manwaringe, one of the Gentle-
    men Ushers of the Kinges majesties Chamber,
    for him selfe, a yoman Usher, fower yomen, two
    gromes of the saied Chamber, one grome of the
    Wardrobe, and a Grome porter, for makinge ready
    at the Kinges Palaice at Westm^r by the space of
    fower daies, for every of them, as apperith by
    a bill signed with the Lorde Chamberlein's hand,
    the some of   .   .   .   .   iiij^{li}

Monethes Wages in November.

Item to Richard Cicell, yoman of the Kinges robes   xxx^s

Ordenary Paymentes in December, 2 *Edw. VI.*

Sondaye at Westminster.

Item for the Kinges offeringe on X͞pcmas daie .   .   nil.

Item to the Children of the Kinges Chappell, for a
rewarde for singinge *gloria in excelsis* on X͞pemas
daie   .   .   .   .   xl˙

Item to the Kinges Harroldes at Armes, for their
largesse on Christcmas daye   .   .   .   .   cˢ

Item for the Kinges daily Almese this weke   .   .   xxxvij˙ xj͏ᵈ

Item paied to Robert Olyver, Deputie to Sir William
Cavendishe, knighte, Thresaurer of the Kinges
Maᵗᵉˢ Chamber, beinge attendaunte alwaies at the
Court upon the Kinges most honorable Counsaile,
for his costes and charges, &c. .   .   .   .   ixˡⁱ

Item to Edmonde Pigeon for his charges, for him selfe
and his man, hieringe of horses at Otelandes, to
the More, and to Grenewiche, for the delyvery of
Stuffe to the Lady Elizabeth her graces officers, &c.   .   .   .   .   .

Item paied to Nicholas Foskewe and Edwarde Corne-
walles, the Kinges majesties grome porters, for
so moche money by them disbursed for provisyon
of grene bowes for the Kinges majesties previe
Chamber, and the Lorde Protectours Lodginges
at Hamptoncourte, viz., iiijᵒʳ loodes, and for
Six Loodes for like cause at Otelandes, making
in all x loodes at ij˙ iiij͏ᵈ the Loode, for cariadge
and cuttinge of the same .   .   .   .   .   xxiij˙ iiij͏ᵈ

Item paied to John Ventrixe, the Kinges maᵗᵉˢ fermor
at Saint James, for house rome there for the
office of the Kinges beddes by the space of one
weke   .   .   .   .   ij˙

Item paied to Sir John Markham, knighte, Liewtenant

of the Tower of London, for the Diettes and
other necessaries of Edwarde Courteney and his
man for fower monethes. . . . xxj^{li} xij^s

Item paied to William Lorde Marquus of Northampton, master of the Kinges majesties Hawkes, by
vertue of the Kinges warrant dated the xxvth
day of Marche . . . . . . iiij^{xx}x^{li}

Item paied to Richard Cooke, Richard Skynner, Henry
Hariot, Thamas Sowthey, and John Birche,
the Kinges ma^{tes} Plaiers, by vertue of the K.'s
warrant dated the xxiiijth day of December,
Anno R. Edw. vj^{u} Secundo, conteyning the payment of lxvj^s viij^d by the yere to every of them
duringe their lyves . . . . xvj^{li} xiij^s iiij^d

Item paied to Thomas Bill, Docter of Phisicke, being
unpaied for a yere and a halfe, viz. from our Lady
day A^o R. Edw. sexti primo, until Michaelmas
Anno R. pred. Secundo, both quarters accompted,
after the rate of l^{li} by yere, the some lxxv^{li}

Quarter's Wages.

Item to Sir John Markham, knight, liewtenante of
the tower of London . . . . . xxv^{li}

Item to him more, for fyndinge of poore prysoners xxv^{li}

Item paied to Sir William Pawlet, knight, Lorde grete
M^r and Chief Justice of the Kinges Maeisties
forestes on this side Trente, for his halfe yeres fee
dewe at this present Christemas . . . l^{li}

Item to Cornelis Zifridus, Docter of phisicke withe the
Lady Anne Cleves grace . . . . xj^{li} xiij^s iiij^d

Item to Sir Thomas Paston, knight, Keper of the long
gallery at Grenewiche . . . . xvj^{li} xiii^s iiij^d

Item to Thomas Peryn and John Peryn, Kepers of the
    Kinges Majesties beares   .   .   .   .   lvij^s q^r·di.

Item to Richard Darryngton, M^r of the Kinges ma^{tie}
    mastyves, and his servant under him   .   .   Cvj^s v^d ob.

Item to John Heiwood, placr of the virginalles   .   l^s

Item to Robert Hinstocke and George Birche, plaiers
    of enterludes   .   .   .   .   .   xxxiij^s iiij^d

Item to Anthony Totto, painter   .   vj^{li} v^s

Item to Bartholomew Penne, painter   .   .   vj^{li} v^s

Item to misteris Levin Terlinge, paintrixe   x^{li}

Item to Richard Atzile, graver of stones   C^s

Item to Sir Percyvall Harte, knight   .   .   C^s

Item to Helinor Hutton, widowe   .   .   .   xxxiij^s iiij^d

Item to Sir Richard Bawdewine, preiste   xlv^s viij^d

Item to Edmonde Mody, gent.   .   .   .   xv^s ij^d

Item to Elizabeth Darrell, gentlewoman   l^s

Item to Sir William Herbert, knight   xj^{li} xiij^s iiij^d

Item to John Amadas, yoman   .   .   .   xlv^s vij^d ob.

Item to Sir Thomas Paston, knight   xj^{li} xiij^s iiij^d

Item to Elizabeth, Lady Kildare   xxxiij^{li} vj^s viij^d

Item to Nicholas Stewarde al. Allen, scoller   xxxiij^s iiij^d

Item to John Belmaine, teacher to the Kinges Matie
    for the frenche tonge   .   .   .   .   xj^{li} xiij^s iiij^d

Item to Sir William Cavendishe, knight, Treasurer
    of the Kinges Chamber   .   .   .   .   xxv^{li}

Item more for his Diettes   .   .   .   xxv^{li}

Item for his Clerkes under him   .   .   .   C^s

Item more for his bootchier   .   .   .   l^s

Item for necessaries in his saied office   .   .   l^s

Item to John Cary, paym^r of Hunesdon   iiij^{li} xj^s iij^d

Item to Robert Colson, songpricker, for one half yere,
    dewe at this Christemas   .   .   .   xl^s

Item paied to Frauncis Knolles esquier   .   .   xl^s

Item to John Nowell, scolm^r to the Ks. Henchemen   C^s

Item to Thomas Preston, gent. . . . . lxvj^s viij^d
Item to Willm Phelippes, writer . . . . l^s
Item to Stephen Vaughan, writer . . . . c^s
Item to Nichãs Bacon, studeant at the lawe l^s
Item to Petrus Olivarus, writer . . . . c^s
Item to Sir William Penyson, knight . . . x^{ll}
Item to Christofer Mounte, stranger . . . c^s
Item to Galterus Delenus, stranger . . . cxvj^s viij^d
Item to Nichãs de Modeno, stranger . . . cv^s
Item to Florentius Diaceto, stranger . . . xvij^{ll} x^s
Item to Jasper Gaffoyne, Italion . . . cxvj^s viij^d
Item to Sigewalte Fredricke, stranger . vj^{ll} xiij^s iiij^d
Item to Deago de Cayes, spanyerd . . . . vij^{ll} x^s
Item to Done Michael Vives de Canamas xviij^{ll} xv^s
Item to Frances Haecke and Barbara his wyeff,
    straungers . . . . vj^{ll} v^s
Item to Anthony de Musica, straunger xviij^{ll} xv^s
Item to William Leche, scotisheman . . vj^{ll} v^s
Item to John Barslao, Hungarion . . . xviij^{ll} xv^s
Item to Countie Waldecke, straunger . . . xviij^{li} xv^s
Item to Messio Bruno, Almayne, and his two sonnes,
    for one halfe yeare . . . . . . c^{li}

Rewardes geven to dyvers Persons on Newyersday A. R.
Edw. vj. pred. Secundo.

Item to the Kinges Harroldes at Armes for their
    largesse on Newyersdaye, as hath byn ac-
    customed . . . . . . vj^{ll}
Item to the Still Mynstrells . . . . iiij^{ll}
Item to the New Sagbuttes . . . . . iiij^{ll}
Item to Mr. Thomas Strete, grome . . . xl^s
Item to Mr. Richard Cicell, yoman of the K. robes xl^s
Item to Robert Robotham, grome of the K. robes xl^s
Item to William More, harper . . . . xx^s

Item to Hughe Pallarde, Edwarde Laicke, Thomas
    Alye, Thomas Curson, Robert Maye, Alaine
    Robson, and Thomas Pagington, the Kinges Myn-
    strells, who served his grace when he was Prince   vij^{li}

Item to Richard Bower, M^r of the Children of the
    Kinges Chappell, for playinge before the Kinges
    Majestie with the saied Children   .   vj^{li} xiij^s iiij^d

Item to the Kinges old Vialls   .   .   xxvj^s viij^d

Item to the Kinges new Vialls   .   .   vj^{li}

Item to the gentelmen of the Kinges Chappell   . xiij^{li} vj^s viij^d

Item to Lewes de Bassyam, Anthony de Bassyam,
    Jasper de Bassyam, John de Bassyam, and
    Baptiste de Bassyam, mynstrells, in rewarde   c^s

Item to the Kinges plaiers of Enterludes   .   . vj^{li} xiij^s iiij^d

Item to Guillam de Vait, Guillam de Trope, and
    Pety John, Mynstrelles   .   .   .   iiij

Item to James the footeman, that gave the Kinge
    Lynes and Collers   .   .   .   xl^s

Item to Sir William Rainsforde, knight, and Mr.
    John Norrys, gent. ushers, that gave the Kinge
    twoo dosenies of Napkins, thone doseine garnished
    with golde, and the other with silver   .   . xiij^s iiij^d

Item to the Duchess of Somerset her graces servaunte liij^s iiij^d

Item to Sir Edmond Peckham, knight, his servaunt xiij^s iiij^d

Item to Sir Thomas Hennage, knight, his servant . xx^s

Item to Sir Anthony Selenger, knight, his servaunt . xiij^s iiij^d

Item to Sir Thomas Carden his servaunt   xiij^s iiij^d

Item to Sir Richard Gresham, knight, his servaunt . xiij^s iiij^d

Item to Mr Sackvile, Chauncellor of the Courte of
    augmentations, his servaunt   .   .   . xiij^s iiij^d

Item to Sir Walter Mildmay, knight. his servaunt . xiij^s iiij^d

Item to M. Cheke his servaunt   .   .   . vj^s viij^d

Item paied to Richard Grafton, the Kinges majesties
    printer, in rewarde   .   .   .   . vj^s viij^d

Item to Guydo Calvacant, merchant stranger, who
    gave the King a pece of velvet   xiij^s iiij^d

Item to Reyne Wulff, Stacyoner, his servante, in
    rewarde   .   .   .   .   vj^s viij^d

Item to Sir Dowglasse, the Scottishe preiste, in rewarde   xl^s

Ordenarye Paymentes in Januarye, 2 Edw. VI.

Item paied to William Griffithe, Keper of the Kinges
    stondinge warderobe at Richemounte, for the
    wages of fyve Arresmen, working and mendinge
    of certaine olde hanginges brought from Notting-
    ham to serve at Richemounte aforesaied, every of
    them by the space of iiij^{xx} and xvj dayes, at viij^d
    the daye   .   .   .   .   .   .   xviij^{li} xviij^s viij^d

Monethes Wages.

Item to Richard Cicell, yoman of the Robes   xxxj^s

Item to Nichās Puvall, Mynstrell   .   .   .   xlj^s iiij^d

Item to Alexander Pennaxe, Drumslade   xxxj^s

By Warrant.

Item paied to William Cholmeley, Coferer to the
    Lady Anne Cleve her grace, by vertue of the
    Kinges majesties warrante dormant for the pay-
    ment of certaine and sondry her graces officers,
    gentelmen, and Gentelwomen quarterly, for one
    quarter fully ronne at Christemas last paste, the
    somme of   xxx

Ordenarye Payementes in Februarye, 3 Edw. VI.

Monethes Wages.

Item to Alexander Pennaxe, Drumslad   .   .   .   xxviij^s

Item to Richard Cicell, yoman of the Kinges robes   .   xxviij^s

Paymentes by Warrantes.

Item paied to tharchedeacon of Richemounte, by
virtue of a decree dormant out of the Courte of
Generall Surveiors, for one yere fully ronne at the
feast of Saint Mighell Tharchangell last past, the
somme of .   .   .   .   lxxvj^s iiij^d

Item paied to Mr Edwarde Vaughan, Capitaine of
Portesmouthe, by vertue of the Kinges warrant
dormant, for him selfe, his Capitaigne, pety capitaigne, and c. Sonldiers, for one hole yere, &c. .   D^{li}

Ordenarye Payementes in Marche, 3 Edw. VI.

Sondaye at Westm^r.

Item to Mr Josephe, for preachinge before the Kinges
majestie this Sondaye   .   .   .   .   .   xx^s

Sondaye at Westm^r.

Item to master Ayer for preachinge, &c.   xx^s

Sondaye at Westm^r.

Item to Docter Parker for preachinge, &c.   xx^s

Sondaye at Westm^r.

Item to maister Curtoppe for preachinge, &c.   xx^s

Item for the Kinges daily Almese this weke   xxxvij^s xj^d

Item to Phelip Androwes, the under Marshall of the
Kinges Marshalsie, for chardges of him selfe and
three men gevinge attendaunce upon Capitaine
Jerimono, Cecilion, a straunger, by the counsailes
commaundement, by the space of xij daies in the
moneth of Nov. laste, &c.   .   .   .   .   vj^{li} xiij^s iiij^d

Item paied to Sir William Rainsforde, knighte,

gentcl. Usher of the K's ma^{tes} Chamber, for him
selfe, twoo yomen, and iiij^{or} gromes, for makinge
readye the Parliament House by the space of 6
daies in the monethe of Nov. last, &c.   cvj^s

Item paied to the said Sir Willm Rainsforde, gent.
Usher, &c. for certaine necessary charges by him
bought, &c. and for makinge ready and givinge
attendaunce at prorogation tyme of the Parliament by the space of sixe daies: And also for
his bourdewages duringe the Parliament tyme,
that is to saie begynninge the xth day of Nov. A^o
secundo Reg. Edw. vj^u, and endinge the last day
of December following, &c.   .   .   .   .   xix^{li} ij^s x^d

Monethes Wages.

Item to Philip van Welder, luter	lxvj^s viij^d
Item to Peter van Welder, luter . . . _.	xxxj^s
Item to William Moore, harper	xxxj^s
Item to Thomas Kent, singingeman . . .	xv^s vj^d
Item to Thomas Bonde, singingeman . . .	xv^s vj^d
Item to John Severnake, rebecke . . .	xlj^s iiij^d
Item to Hanse Hosenet, viall	xxxiij^s iiij^d
Item to Albert de Venice, viall	lj^s viij^d
Item to Ambrose de Millano, viall	lj^s viij^d
Item to Vincent de Venice, viall	lj^s viij^d
Item to Fraunces de Venice, viall	lj^s viij^d
Item to Marke Anthony Galiardell, viall . . .	lj^s viij^d
Item to George de Combre, viall	lj^s viij^d
Item to Marke Anthony, sagbut	xlj^s iiij^d
Item to Anthony Mary, sagbut	xlj^s iiij^d
Item to Nicholas Androwe, sagbut	xlj^s iiij^d
Item to Anthony Symonde, sagbut	xlj^s iiij^d
Item to Richd Woodward, plaier on the bagpipe .	xx^s viij^d

Item to Nicholas Puvall, mynstrell   xlj^s iiij^d
Item to Hughe Pallarde, mynstrell .   .   .   .   xxxj^s
Item to Edward Laecke, mynstrell .   .   .   .   xxxj^s
Item to Thomas Alye, mynstrell   .   .   .   .   xxxj^a
Item to Thomas Curson, mynstrell   .   .   .   xxxj^s
Item to Robert Maye, mynstrell   xxxj^s
Item to Allaine Robson, mynstrell .   .   .   .   xxxj^s
Item to Thomas Pagington, mynstrell   .   .   .   xxxj^s
Item to Alexander Pennaxe, drumslade .   .   .   xxxj^s
Item to the Children of the Kinges ma^{tes} Chappell
    for their bourdwages   .   .   .   xxvj^s viij^d
Item to Richard Cicell, yoman of the Robes   xxxj^s
Item to Phelip Clampe, faulconer .   .   .   .   lxij^s
Item to Richard Cattelin, Keeper of the Ks. ponds   xv^s vj^d
Item to the same Richard Catteline, &c. for his livery
    cote, dewe at our Lady daye .   .   .   .   xxij^s vj^d

Payement by Warrant.

Item to John Banester, Esquier, master of the Ks.
    Ma^{tes} Toiles, by vertue of the Kinges warrant
    dormaunte, conteyning the payement yerely unto
    him of c markes during his lief, &c.   lxvj^{li} xiij^s iiij^d

Quarter's Wage

Item Sir John Markham, knight, lieutenant of the
    Tower .   .   .   .   xxv^{li}
Item to him more for fyndinge pore prisoners   xxv^{li}
Item to xv yomen attending at the said Tower   .   xxxiiij^{li} v^s
Item to Thomas Bill, phisicion   .   .   .   .   xij^{li} x^s
Item to Docter Benteley, phisicion .   .   .   .   x^{li}
Item to Docter Huicke, phisicion   .   l^s
Item to Cornelis Zifridus, docter of phisicke   .   xj^{li} xiij^s iiij^d
Item to Nichās Crasier, Astronomer   .   c^s

Item to John de Sodo, Potycarye . . . . vj^{li} xiij^s iiij^d

Item to Thomas Alsop, Potycarye . . . . vj^{li} xiij^s iiij^d

Item to John Emyngway, Potycarye . . . lv^s viij^d ob.

Item to Thomas Vycary, Surgeon . . . . c^s

Item to John Aliff, Surgeon . . . . vij^{li} x^s

Item to Richard Ferres, Surgeon . . . . c^s

Item to Nichãs Alcocke, Surgeon . . . . l^s

Item to George Hollande, Surgeon . . . . l^s

Item to Thomas Gemynous, Surgeon . . . l^s

Item to Henry Forreste, Surgeon . . . . x^{li}

Item to Henry Makerethe, Surgeon . . . . x^{li}

Item to William lorde Marcus of Northampton, M^r
of the Kinges majesties Hawkes . . x^{li}

Item to Sir Anthony Kingston, knight, sergiante of
the Kinges Hawkes, for one halfe yere, &c. xviij^{li} v^s

Item to John Peryn, sergeant of the Kinges beares lvij^s q^r

Item to Richard Darrington. M^r of the Kinges Mas-
tives, and his servaunt under him . . cvj^s v^d ob.

Item to William Beaton, Organ maker . . c^s

Item to John Heiwood, plaier on the virginalles l^s

Item to Barnarde de Ponte, harper . . . . c^s

Item to Robert Reynolds, Welsh mynstrell, for halfe
a yere . . . . xxxiij^s iiij^d

Item to Robert Hinstocke and George Birche xxxiij^s iiij^d

Item to Anthony Totto, painter . . vj^{li} v^s

Item to Barthilmew Penne, painter . . . . vj^{li} v^s

Item to Misteris Levin Terlinge, paintrixe x^{li}

Item to Richard Atzile, graver of Stones . . . c^s

Item to Sir Thomas Paston, knight . . . xj^{li} xiij^s iiij^d

Item to Elizabeth Lady Kildare . . . xxxiij^{li} vj^s viij^d

Item to Richard Moryson, gent. . . . . c^s

Item to Sir William Cavendishe, knight, Treasorer
of the Chamber . . . . . . xxv^{li}

Item to him more for his diettes . . . . xxv^{li}

Item to him more for his Clerkes under him	C^{s}
Item more for his Bootehier	[illegible]
Item more for his necessaries in his s^{d} office	[illegible]
Item to Fruncis Knolles, esquier	x^{li}
Item to Thomas Preston, gent.	lxvj^{s} viij^{d}
Item to Nichās Bacon, studeant at the lawe	l^{s}
Item to Petrus Olivarus, writer	C^{s}
Item to Thomas Carew, gent.	C^{s}
Item to Richard Coke, enterlude plaier	xvj^{s} viij^{d}
Item to Richard Skynner, enterlude plaier . .	xvj^{s} viij^{d}
Item to Henry Hariot. enterlude plaier	xvj^{s} viij^{d}
Item to Thomas Sowthey, enterlude plaier	xvj^{s} viij^{d}
Item to John Birche, enterlude plaier .	xvj^{s} viij^{d}

Halfe yeres Wages.

Item to the lady Anne Graye	vj^{li} xiij^{s} iiij^{d}
Item to Sir John Russell, lorde prevy Scale	x^{li}j xiij^{s} iiij^{d}
Item to Sir Richard Candishe, knight . . .	C^{s}
Item to Sir Edmonde Peckham, knight .	x^{li} x^{s}
Item to Edwarde Mountagewe, Lorde Chiefe justice of the Common Place	
Item to George Lorde Baron Hadecke .	lxx^{li}
Item to Sir John Guildeforde, knight . . .	xiij^{li} vj^{s} viij^{d}
Item to Edw. Harvell, Ambassador in Venice	l^{li}

Payment by Warrant.

Item to Edward Coltherste, by vertue of the Kinges generall Surveyors letters, for so moche money to him geven for his paines takinge in writinge cciiij^{or} Letters, for the callinge in of the Kinges Dettes	lvj^{s} viij^{d}

Ordenarye Payementes in Apryll, 3 Edw. VI.

Palme Sondaye at West^r.

Item for the Kinges offeringe this Sondaye	nil cā predicta
Item for the Kinges daily Almese this weke	xxxvij^s xj^d
Item to Docter Coxe, for preachinge before the Kinges Majestie this Sondaye	xx^s

Maundye Thursday at Westm^r.

Item geven to xij poore men at tha Kinges Maundye the same daye, every of them xij^d in a purse .	xij^s
Item to the saied xij pore men everye of them xx^s in a purse, by waye of the Kinges ma^{tes} rewarde, in stede of his Ma^{tes} maundy gowne .	xij^{li}
Item for ij doseine of purses to put the saied money in	iij^s iiij^d
Item for the Kinges offering this goodfriday	nil ut supra.

Easter daye at Grenewiche.

Item for the Kinges offeringe at the resurrection	nil cā pred.
Item for the Kinges offeringe at Highmas .	xiij^s iiij^d
Item for the Kinges daily Almese this weke .	xxxvij^s xj^d
Item to the Kinges Haroldes at Armes for their largesse on Easter daye	c^s
Item to the Kinges Cookes for a rewarde the same daye	vj^{li} xiij^s iiij^d
Item for the Kinges Harroldes at Armes for their largesse on Saint Georges daye	c^s
Item paied to Hughe Lee, Clerke of tharmorye at Grenewiche, to thandes of John Kele his Deputie, for sixe monethes wages of the Almaigne Armorers, &c.	clxxiij^{li} vj^d
Item paied to Docter Coxe, the Kinges majesties Almoyner, for to distrybute on Palme Sondaye and the weke followinge emongest pore parisshes,	

as appereth by the Kinges Counsailles War-
raunte   .   .   .   .   Cxxxiij^{li} vj^s viij^d

Item paied by vertue of the Kinges Majesties war-
raunte, dated at Somerset place the fyrste daye
of Aprill in the yere of our Lorde God one
thowsand fyve hundreth fourtie and nyen, to
seventene of the K's Watermen for their wages
and lyveryes for one hole yere ended at Christemas in the seconde yere of the reigne of our saied
Soveraigne Lorde Kinge Edwarde the Sixte;
that is to saye, to every of them for their wages
fourtie Shillinges, and to every of them for their
lyveries twenty twoo shillinges and sixe pence.
Item paied more by vertue of the same warrante
to the wyves of thurtene watermen whiche
perryshed and dyed upon the Seas, for their
wages for half a yere ended at Midsommer last,
in the seconde yere of our saied Sovereigne
lordes reigne, every of them twentie shillinges,
the somme of thurteene poundes. Item paied
more to the forsaied seventene Watermen for
their wages for one quarter of a yere ended at
our lady daye in the yere of our lorde God one
thowsande fyve hundreth fourtie and nyen
aforesaid; that is to saye, to every of them tenne
shillinges, the some of eight poundes and tenne
shillinges. Item paid by vertue of the said warrante to thurteene other Watermen, lately admitted to serve in the places of the said thurtene
deceassed; that is to saye, to every of them for
their lyveries, for one hole yere ended at Christemas in the saied second yere of our Sovereigne
Lorde Kinge Edwarde the Sixte, twentie-two
Shillinges and Sixe pence.   And for their wages

for thre quarters of a yere ended at our Lady daye
laste in the saied yere of our Lorde God one
thowsand fyve hundreth fourtie and nyen, to
every of them thurtie Shillinges, the somme of
Nientene poundes and tene shillinges.   In thole   cviij^{li} xv^s
Item to Sir William Rainsforde, knight, gent. Usher
of the Parliament house, for his bourdwages and
for dyvers emptions by him provided for the
saied Parliament House, as apperith by a bill,
the some of . . . .   xx^{li} ij^s vj^d

Monethes Wages in Apryll.

Item to Philip van Welder, luter	lxvj^s viij^d
Item Peter van Welder, luter	xxx^s
Item to Will'm Moore, harper	xxx^s
Item to Thomas Kent, Singingman . . .	xv^s
Item to Thomas Bowde, Singingman . . .	xv^s
Item to Alexaunder Penaxe, Drumslade . . .	xxx^s
Item to the Children of the Kinges majesties chappell for their bourdwages	xxvj^s viij^d
Item to Richard Cicell, yoman of the Roobes	xxx^s

Payment by Warrant.

Item paied to Sr Thomas Darcey, knight, M^r of the
Kinges Armory, by vertue of the Kinges warrant
dated the firste day of Aprill, A° Regis Edw.
sexti pred. tercio, for so moche money to be by
him employed aboute the byinge of Gownes,
Cootes, and Dublets; that is to saie, for xxiv
Armerers and other officers belonging to the
saied Armorye, to every of them iiij^{or} yardes of
brode cloth for a gowne, price every yarde v^s;
and to every of them iij yardes of Karsey for a
Dublet and a payre of hose, at ij^s the y^{de}, in full
payment of the same warrante, the Somme of   xxxj^{li} iiij^s

Ordenarye Paymentes in Maye, 3 *Edw. VI.*

Item paied to Sir John Markham, knight, Liewte-
naunte of the Tower of London, for the Diettes
and other necessaries of Edward Courteney and
his man remayninge within the saied Tower of
London, for sixe monethes, &c.   .   .   .   xxxij^{li} viij^s

Item paied to Edmonde Pigeon, Clerke of the Kinges
Majesties Gwarderobes, &c.   .   .   .   .   xxiij^s

Monethes wages.

Item to Richard Cicell, yoman of the roobes   xxxj^s
Item to Cleoment Harleston, ostringer   .   xxxj^s

Payment by warrant.

Item paied to William Cholmeley, Coferer to the
Lady Anne Cleve her graces housholde, by vertue of the Kinges majesties Warrante dormante
for the payment of certaine her graces officers,
gentelmen, and gentelwomen attendinge, &c.   xxx

Ordenarye Paymentes in June, 3 *Edw. VI.*

Item paied to Robert Olyver, Deputie to Sir Wittm
Cavendishe, knight, Thresaurer of the Kinges
Majesties moste honorable Chamber, being attendaunte alwaies upon the Kinges moste honorable Counsaille, for his costes and chardges, being
sent at dyvers and sondrye tymes for money from
the Courte within the monethes of Januarye,
Februarye, Marche, Aprill, Maye, and June, &c.   vj^{li}

Item paied to thurtie of the Kinges Majestie his
Watermen, for their wages for one quarter of
a yere, &c.   .   .   .   .   xv^{li}

Paymentes by Warrante.

Item paied to Nicholas Uvedale, scolemaster to Mr. Edward Courteney, beinge within the Tower of London, by vertue of the Kinges Majesties warrante, &c. . . . . lxvj^s viij^d

Quarters Wages at Mydsomer.

Item to William Beaton, Organmaker . . . c^s
Item to John Heywood, plaier on the virginalles l^s
Item to Barnard de pont, Harper . . .
Item to Robt. Hinstocke and George Birche, plaiers xxxiij^s iiij^d
Item to Piro Guye, plaier on the fluit . vij^{li} xij^s j^d
Item to Richard Cooke, enterlude plaier . xvj^s viij^d
Item to Richard Skynner, enterlude plaier . . xvj viij^d
Item to Henry Hariot, enterlude plaier . . . xvj^s viij^d
Item to Thomas Sowthey, enterlude plaier . . xvj^s viij^d
Item John Birche, enterlude plaier . . . xv ^{s} viij^d
Item to Piro Doulxe, frenche Cooke . . . xvj^s viij^d
Item to Hugh Pigot, Cooke . . . . . xxx^{s}v ^{d}
Item to Edward Wilken, Mr Cooke for the Hall place, for half a yere due this Mydsomer . x^{li}
Item to Richard Currey, Mr Cooke for the Kinges mouthe, for half a yere . . . . . xv^{li}
Item to Anthony Totto, painter . . . . vj^{li} v^s
Item to Barthilmewe Penne, painter . . . vj^{li} v^s
Item to Misteris Levin Terlinge, paintrixe . x^{li}
Item to Richard Atzile, graver of stones . c^s
Item to Nich^{as} Bacon, studeant at the lawe l^s
Item paied to Sir William Penison, Kt., straunger x^{li}
Item to Galterus de Levins, stranger . . cxvj^s viij^d
Item to Anthony de Musica, straunger . . . xviij^{li} xv^s
Item to John de Founteney alias Berteville, Frencheman . . . . xxxvij^{li} x^s

Item to Countie Waldecke, straunger　.　.　.　　xviij^{li} xv^s

Item to Messio Bruno, Almaigne, for himself and his
twoo sonnes, &c.　.　.　.　.　.　.　　c^{li}

Item to Robert Colson, Songprycker, &c.　　　xl^s

Ordenarye Paymentes in Julye, 3 Edw. VI.

Monethes Wages.

Item to Richard Cicell, yoman of the Roobes　　　xxxj^s

Item to Alexander Pennaxe, Drumslade　　　　xxxj^s

Item to Richard Johnson, Keper　.　.　.　.　　xx^s viij^d

Item to Robert Hemynge, gunner　.　.　.　.　　xv^s vj^d

Ordenarye Payementes in August, 3 Edw. VI.

By Warrantes.

Item paied to John Starkeye, the Kinges fletcher, by
vertue of the Kinges Warrante dated the xvijth
daye of June, &c. for so moche money to be by
him employed for ciij Sheves of Arrowes and
Girdells, at v^s iiij^d every of them, with their
Cases, &c.　.　.　.　.　.　.　.　xxvij^{li} ix^s iiij^d

Item paied to Capitaiene Cleen van Bruen, Almaigne,
by vertue of the Kinges Counsailles Letter
dated the xth day of Auguste, &c. for the wages
of certaine Almaines, paied for a monethe afore-
hande, &c.　.　.　.　.　.　.　ccccxlv^{li} xv^s x^d

Item paied to Capitinge Vansall van Ardenbrug, by
vertue of the Kinges Counsailles Letters dated the
xth of August, &c. for the wages of certaine
Almaignes, for a monethe beforehande, &c.　　ccclx^{li} ij^s viij^d

Item paied to Capitaigne Henry Hartforde, Almaigne,
by vertue of the Kinges Counsailles Letter dated
the xiij day of Auguste, &c. for the wages of

certaine Almaynes being iiij^{c}xx horsemen of his
trayne untill the xxiiijth day of this monethe &c.   м.ccviij^{li} vj^s

Item paied to Captaignes Clain van Brewen & William
Vaderton in preste by vertue of the Kinges Counsailes Letter dated the xiiijth daye of Auguste
A° 1549 for the payment of certaine Almaignes
their wages to be defaulked apon their next
monethes paye, to either of them C^{li} a pece for
September in full payment of the same &c.   cc^{li}

Ordenarye Paymentes in Sept. 3 Edw. VI.

Item to Allaine Bawdyson, clockemaker, by vertue of
the Ks. warrant under his prevye signet dated at
the palaice of Westm^r the thurde daye of Aprill
A° Regis Edwardi sexti iij^{cio} the wages or fee of
viij^d by daye which Sebestian Lysney, clockemaker, late enjoyed &c.   .   .   .   .   .   xij^{li} iiij^s

Item paied to Willm Knighteley, gunner, by vertue of
the Kinges warrante &c. the wages of vj^d by the
daye, which Richard Golde, gunner, late had *
&c.   .   .   .   .   xlix^s

Quarters Wages.

Item to John Heiwood, plaier on the Virginalles	l^s
Item to Nichās Stewarde, al Allen, scoler	xxxiij^s iiij^d
Item to Fraunces Knolles, esquier . . .	x^{li}
Item to John Nowell scole m^r to the K's henchemen .	c^s
Item to Thomas Preston, gent.	lxvj^s viij^d
Item to Nichās Vuedale, instructor to Mr Courteney	lxvj^s viij^d
Item to Nichās Bacon, studeant at lawe	l^s

* Accordingly in the list of gunners we find the name of Richard Golde, but against
his name is written " *Nil quia non sol.*"

Halfe yeres wages.

Item to the Ladye Anne Graye . . vj^{li} xiij^s iiij^d

Item to Sir Richard Candishe, Knight . c^s

Item to Edwarde Mountagewe, lord cheif Justice of
the Common place . . . . . l^s

Item to Sir John Guilforde, Knight, Chamberleine
to the Lady Anne Cleve her grace xiij^{li} vj^s viij^d

Item paied to Richard Hogge, footeman to the Lady
Marye her grace . . . . . . vij^{li} ij^d

Item to Mr Harvell, the Kinges majesties Ambassador
in Venice . . . . l^{li}

Paymentes by Warrant.

Item paied to the Capitaines William Vanne Walder-
ton and Clyen van Brewne, Almaignes, &c. in
preste for the payement of Wages of certaine
Almaignes, &c. . . . . . . Mlv^{li} xvij^s viij^d

Item paied to Barthilmew Fortune, merchaunte of the
Citie of Florence &c. for saltepeter by him solde
to the Kinges Majestie &c. . . . . c^{li}

Item paied to Sir John Mason, Knighte, Master of the
Kinges majesties Postes, for somoche money by
him disburced to Postes, Currors, and messengers,
and for dyvers and sondry passages made betwene
Dover and Calice for the conveyinge of the
Kinges ma^{tes} Letters, as by a Boke subscribed
withe his owne hand more plainlye may
appere . . . . . . MDCCCCXV^{li} xviij^s

Om^a of all the Paymentes made from the laste daye of
September A^o Regis Edwardi sexti Secundo untyll
the fyrste daye of Octobre A^o regni Regis Ed-
wardi Sexti predict. tertio . xviij^{ml}xxxvj^{li} ij^s iij^d ^{qa} dl. *

---

* These figures are in the hand-writing of Sir William Cavendish, who seems to have
cast up the different items in the book.

The Office of the Thresaurer of the Quenes Majesties Chamber.[a]   A.D. 1
viij° Marcij Anno primo Mariæ Reginæ.

A breiff abstracte or estymate what is due within the said offyce
at the feaste of Thannuncyac'on of our blessed Lady the
Virgen next comynge.

Ordenary paymentes paiable monethly.

Fyrste due and owing unto the Queene's Highnes

Trumpeters	ccclviij[li] xiij[s] iiij[d]
To the Lewtiers	clv[li] vj[s] viij[d]
To the Harpers	iiij[li] x[s]
To the Singers	liiij[li]
To the Rebeckes.	iiij[xx li]
To the Vyalles	iiij[c]xv[li]
To the Sagbuttes	cccxl[li]
To the Bagpipes	xxxij[li] x[s]
To the Mynstrelles	cccciiij[xx li]
To the Drumslades	xxxvj[li]
To the M[r] of the children of the chappell for their bourdwages	xxx[li] xiij[s] iiij[d]
To divers Yomen	cc[li]
To thoffycers of the Toilles	l[li]
To the Archers	cx[li]
To the faulconers	ccclx[li]
To the takers of pheasauntes and partridges	xxv[li]
To the gromes of the Quenes Buckhoundes for houndes' meate	xviij[li] xvj[s] x[d]
To the Kepers of Waltham Forest	cclxx[li]

---

[a] Mary ascended the throne on the 6th July, 1553, and filled it alone until 25th July,
1554. Lady Jane Grey had assumed the crown on the 6th July, and continued to be
called Queen by her supporters until the 17th of the same month. Sir W. Cavendish's
accounts contain no notice of her usurpation, but he was continued in the place of
Treasurer of the Chamber under Mary, and under Philip and Mary. This is from the

To the Kepers of Pondes . . . . . xxviij^{li}

To Artyfycers . . . . . cc^{li}

To the Gunners . . . . . DCClx^{li}

To the Deane of the Chappell for the K's and Quene's offeringes cc^{li}

The Quene's highnes daily Almese lxxv^{li} xvj^s viij^d

The Quene's Almese on Maundy Thursday next
     comyng . . . . . . clxxviij^{li} xix^s xj^d

The prevye Almese . . . . . . MDCCC^{li}

The Almayne Armorers at Grenewiche . . . CCCCxxij^{li} v^s

The Clerke of the Checke for house wine iiij^{li}

Dyvers ordenary rewardes paiable at dyvers tymes in the yere   c^{li}

To Preachers in Lent in rewarde . . . . xxj^{li}

To the Haroldes at armes for their Largesse . . lxx^{li}

To Gent. Ushers, Sewers, yomen, gromes, and pages of
     the quenes chamber, Offycers of the Jewelhouse
     and warderobe of beddes, Sergeaunts at Armes,
     Harbengers, the grome porter, and sutch other by
     their billes signed with the Councelles handes DClxvj^{li} xiij^s iiij^d
                                       by estymacon.

To the M^r of the Barges . . . . . cxl^{li}

To the Messengers and others for their Rydinges MM^{li}
                                         by estymation.
                         MMviij^cvj^{li} xiij^s iiij^d

     The certeinty that is owing unto these persons is not yet knowen, for
that the greater nomber of their billes were never yet seen in thoffyce.^a
                         xxv^mDClxxiiij^{li} x^s viij^d ob.

     Ordenary Paymentes paiable quarterly and half yerelie.

To Sir John Markeham, Sir Arthure Darcey, and Sir Edwarde

volume in Sir W. C. Trevelyan's possession, on the cover of which is written, " The boke
of the Copies of the Certyficat made to the Kinges Ma^{tes} Counsell," which extends from
19 Feb. 37° H. VIII., to 24 October 2°-3° Philip and Mary, and from which extracts have
been already given.

     ^a It was part of the complaint of Sir W. Cavendish that he was required to make pay-
ments of bills which were never sent in to his department.

Warner, Knightes, late Lieutenauntes of the Tower of London,
with the dyettes of M^r. Courteney . . iiij^{c}iiij^{xx}v^{ll}

To the xv yomen wayters at the said towre . cv^{ll} viij^s iiij^d

To the Cheiffe Justices of all the Quenes Forestes c^{ll}

To Phisicions and Artstronymers . . . . xxvij^{ll} x^s

To Potycaries . . . . . xxj^{ll} xiij^s vj^d ob.

To Surgeons . . . . cclxvij^{ll} x^s

To offycers of the Leashe . . . . . vij^{ll} x^s

To offycers of the Huntes . . . cxliij^{ll} vj^s iiij^d ob.

To Faulconers . . . . . cclxij^{li} x^s vij^d ob.

To Kepers of howses, parkes, and gardenis iiij^{xx}xvj^{ll} x^s x^d

To Kepers of Beares and Mastyves xviij^{ll} iiij^s xj^d

To Kepers of phesuntes and partridges . xxij^{ll} xvj^s iiij^d

To plaiers on Instrumentes and enterludes cccclviij^{li} x^s v^d

To painters . . . . . iiij^{xx}xvj^{ll} vs.

To Artyfycers . . . cxxxiiij^{li} xj^s iij^d

To dyvers persons for their annuities Mix^{c}xliiij^{ll} vj^s v^d ob.

To Cookes . . . . . . iiij^{xx}xiij^{ll} v^s

To Footemen . . . . . ccclxxvj^{ll} xiij^s iiij^d

To learned men and writers . . . iiij^{xx}xvij^{li} iij^s iiij^d

The Ladye Anne Cleves houshould ccxxxiij^{ll} vj^s viij^d

The offycers of the Jewelhouse . . . . ix^{ll} vj^s viij^d

To gentelmen ushers and Sewers . . . . . xxxv^{ll}

To watermen . . . . xliij^{ll}

To Straungers . . . Mviij^{c}lviij^{li} iiij^s x^d

To the yomen of the garde extraordynary in iiij^d
    by daye . . . . . MMCCCiiij^{xx}x^{ll} vj^s viij^d

      ,,   ,,   in vj^d by daye MDCix^{ll} xiij^s iiij^d

To Sir John Mason, Knighte, M^r of the Postes MM^l. Yt is
thought he
hath receyved
p'te in other
offyces.

To the M. of the Queene's workes   MMM^{ll}. It is
                                          thoughthehath
                                          receyved it in
                                          other offyces.

Extraordenary Paymentes.

To the Lorde Marchus of Northampton for his dyettes, besides his
   post money not yet knowen ^a   .   cccciiij^{xx}v^{ll}
To Sir Thomas Smythe for his dyettes and poste
   money . . . . . . ccxlviij^{ll} xij^s viij^d
To Docter Olyver for his dyettes and poste money ciiij^{xx}xiiij^{ll} vj^s viij^d
To Sir Gilbert Dethicke, Knighte, principall-King-at-Armes, Chester
   Harraulde at Armes and Rouge Dragon, for their dyettes and
   poste mony . . . . . cccxxxj^{ll} vij^s iiij^d
To Sr John Burthwicke, Knight, late Ambassador in
   Denmarke . . . . . . ccxx^{ll}
To the Quenes Ma^{tes} Fletcher . . . . lxvj^{ll} xiij^s iiij^d
To the Harrouldes at Armes for their dyettes in the
   progresse tyme . . clxviij^{ll} xvj^s viij^d
     Summa Totalis   xxvij^{ml}cciiij^{xx}ix^{ll} vij^s iiij^d ob.

WILL OF JOHN TREVELYAN OF NETTLECOMB.^b

50.

   To all Christian people to whom this present writyng tripartyd
shall come. John Trevelyan of Netelcomb in the Countie of
Somerset, esquyer, sendeth gretyng, in the Lord God Almyghty.
Where as by one other endenture made bitwene me the said John

---

^a This item and some others refer to the "solemn embassage," as Sir John Hayward
calls it, of the Marquis of Northampton, the Bishop of Ely, Sir Philip Hoby, and others,
to the King of France, in order to present him with the order of the Garter "and to treat
with him of other secret affaira." Sir Gilbert Dethick, Garter-King-at-Arms, and other
heralds, accompanied the ambassadors.

^b The indorsement, in a handwriting of the time, is as follows: "An indenture tripartite
made by John Trevylyan of Nettilcomb, Esq., and John Harrys, Serjiant-at-lawe, in anno
5to Ed. Regis vj^{ll}, 1550."

Trevelyan of the one parte, and John Harrys, esquyer, deceasid, late one of the Kynges majestie serjiaunts at law, of the other parte, beryng date the vijth day of Aprell, in the fyfte yere of the raigne of our Soveraigne Lord the Kyng that now is, amonge dyvers and sundry Covenauntes, graunts, and aggrements, had made and concludyd bitwene us aswell concernyng the mariage then to be had bitwene John Trevylian, my son and heire apparent, and Willmote Harrys, doughter of the said John Harrys, as the declaracion of the use and possession of all and syngular Manors, Messuages, landes, tenementes rentes, reversions, suych and other heredytamentes of me the said John Trevelyan, hyt is provyded that hit shall and may be lawfull for me the said Trevylyan to make and declare my last Wyll and testament of all and singuler my said Manors, londes, tenementes, and other hereditamentes, being no parcell of the londes lymytted by the said former endenture for the Joynter of the said Wilmote, nor of the londes appoynted to the said John Harrys for ten yeres, aswell for the preferment of the mariage of my daughters, wherby every of theym with the issues and proffettes therof may be well and truly contentyd and paid of the summe of two hundred markes towardes theire mariage, if they be not otherwyse advauncyd or preferred in my lyef, as for the payment of my lawfull dettes as by the said former indenture more playnely may appere. Know you therfore that the said John Trevylyan being at the makyng of this my last Wyll concernyng the disposicion of all my said Manors, messuages, londes, tenementes, and other hereditamentes not lymyted or appoyntyd for the Joynter of the said Wilmote, nor to the said John Harrys for the terme of ten yeres afore rehersed, in good helth and perfett memorie, lauded be God, and neverthelesse subject to deth most certeyn, the tyme wherof is most uncerteyn, do make and declare my said last Wyll concernyng my said Manors, londes, tenementes, and other hereditamentes not lymyted and appoyntyd as afore is rehersed, in maner and forme folowyng, that is to wete: Ferst, y wyll be[queth] and by these presentes do bequeth unto Mawde my wyef all and synguler my said Manors, mesuages, londes, tenementes, and other hereditamentes not lymitted or appoyntyd as before is rehersed, nor lymyted nor appoyntyd to the Joynture of the said Mawde untyll that she have with the issues and profettes of the same well and truly contentyd and paid all and synguler my lawfull dettes, and, after my said dettes well and truly contented and paid, untyll that she have levyed and recevyd therof the full summe of two hundred markes over and above all charges, and repryses for the preferment of every of my doughters not preferred or advaunced to mariage at the tyme of my deth, if they be maried by the advyse and councell of my said wyeff the same money to be delyvered to my said doughters or theire howsboundes by my said wyef or her executors, at such tyme or tymes as my said wyef shall thynk best or most convenyent. And, if my said wyef shall happyn to dye, which God forbede, before all my said doughters, or any of theym, shall be preferred or advaunced to mariage, then I wyll, and by these presents do bequeth unto Gilys Strongwyse, knight, and John Wadham, esquier, son and heire of Sir Nicholas Wadham, knyght, decessyd, and Baldwyn Hill, clerk, if they be then lyvyng, and to their heires and assignes, as well all and synguler my said Manors, londes, tenementes, and other hereditamentes, appoyntyd unto my said wyef for her Joynture, as all other my said Manors, messuages, londes, tenementes, and other heredytamentes not lymytyd nor appoyntyd as before is rehercyd in the said former endenture, untyll they or theire heires have with the issues and profettes of the same well and truly contentyd and paid all synguler my lawfull dettes not contentyd and paid by my said wyef or her executors. And, after my said dettes well and truly contentyd and paid, untyll they or their heires have recevyd and levyed therof the residue of the two hundred markes not levyed by my said wyef for and towardes the preferment of the mariage of every my said doughters not preferred by my said wyef, if they be maried by the advyse and counsell of the said Sir Gylys, John Wadham, and Baldwyn Hill, or their heires, or the moste parte of theym, the same money to be delyvered and paid to my said doughters or their husbondes at such tyme or tymes as the said Sir Gilys, John Wadham, and Baldwyn Hill, clerk, or their heires, shall thynk best and most convenient by their discressions. In witnesse wherof, to every parte of these endentures I have put my Seale and subscribyd my name, the xth day of August in the fifte yere of the raigne of our Soveraigne Lord, Edward the vjth, by the grace of God of Englond, Fraunce, and Hirlond Kyng, Defender of the faith, and under God of the Church of Englond and also of Irlond the supreme hed.

By me, JOHN TREVELYAN.

L.S.

MAUD TREVELYAN'S JOINTURE.[a]

This Indenture, made the first day of Aprill, in the fyveth yere of the Reigne of our Soveraign Lord Edward the Sixte, by the grace of God of England Fraunce and Ireland Kyng, defendoure of the faith, and of the Church of Ingland and also of Ireland in erth Supreme heed, betwene John Trevilian of Nettilcome in the countie of Somersett, Esquier, of the one partie, and Bartilmewe Combe, of Canyngton, in the said Countie, and Hugh Mill of Heth seint Marie, in the Countie of Devon, gentleman, of the other partie: Witnesseth that it is covenaunted, condiscended, graunted, and agreed betwene the said parties in maner and forme folowing, that is to say: the said John Trevilian, for hym, his heires, and executors, doth covenaunt and graunt to and with the said Bartil- mew and Hugh Hille, that he the said John Trevilian shall in the ƿme of Ester next comyng after the date herof permitte and suffre the said Bartilmew and Hugh to recover by dette of entre in the post, to be pursued by them before the Kynges Justices of his comon

---

[a] This document is Indorsed, " Maude Trevelyan's Junture," in the same hand in which the body of it is written. She was the daughter of Giles Hill, and became the wife of John Trevelyan of Nettlecomb.

pleas at Westminster, ageynst the said John Trevilian, of the manors of Nettilcom, Rowdon, and Wodeaunt, in the said county of Somersett, and all other the mesuages, lands, tenements, and hereditaments of the said John Trevilian in Nettilcom, Rowdon, Woodeaunt, Colton, Chiddesley, Woodhouse, Escott, Capton Vellers, Curden, and Yerd; in the said county of Somersett, to geder with thadvowson of the Church of Nettilcom aforesaid. Thentent, consideration, and very cause of the said recoverie so to be hadde is such that the recoverers, imediatly uppon such recovery hadde and executed, shall stand to be seased of and in all the said maners, mesuages, lands, tenementes, medowes, losenes, pastures, woods, commons, rentes, reversions, and emcions, and all other hereditamentes mentioned in the said recovery, to such uses and intents herafter ensuyng, that is to say, to the use and behove of the said John Trevilian for the terme of his lyfe, without impechement of any wast. And that also the said John Trevilian at all tymes duryng his liff to have full power and auctoritie to make leasses and estates for termè of liff, liffes, or yeres, of the premisses or of any parcell thereof, reservyng uppon every such leasse and estate by hym to be made the olde usuall rentes, as nowe, or at any tyme within this xx yeres last paste, were usually paied and borne for the same. Provided alwayes that these articles last mencioned shall not extend to geve auctoritie to the said John Trevilian to make any leasses of the mansion house and parke of the maner of Nettilcom, nor of the demeanes belongyng to the same, for any longer terme then for his owne liff. And after the deceasse of the said John Trevilian to the use of Mawde Trevilian, now wif of the said John Travilian, duryng the lif of the said Mawde, if the said Mawde doe after the death of the said John Trevilian remayne soole and unmaried, as the saide Mawde by her especiall desire and request hath so desired. And, after the deceasse of the said Mawde Trevilian, or her estate determyned, then to the use of John Trevilian, the sonne and heire apparent of the said John Trevilian the father, and to theires of the bodye of the said John Trevilian the son, lawfully procreate. So that the said John Trevilian the sonne and his heires of his body do permitte and suffre all such leases and grauntes of the premisses or any parte therof to them made by the said John Trevilian the father, as before is mencioned, quietly to hold and enjoy ther interests and estates according to the purporte and tenor of ther seid leasses and grauntes made, without any unlawfull expulsion therof, so the seid lesses be not made without empechement of wast, nor the olde accustomed rentes decayed or mynyshed. And, if it fortune the said John Trevelyan the son to dye without issue of his bodye, then to the use of John Trevilian, second son of the said John Trevilian thelder, and to theyres of his body lawfully procreate, with like proviso and condition for assurance of the interest, and of the lesses and grauntees of the said John Trevilian the father, as before mentioned. And if it fortune the said John Trevilian, the second son, to dye without issue of his body lawfully procreate, then to the use of theires of the body of the said John Trevilian the father; and, for lak of such issue, to the use of the right heires of the said John Trevilian the father for ever, to hold of the chief Lords of the fee by the servys therof due. In witnes herof the parties aforesaid to thes Indentures enterchangeably have putte their seales the day and yere abovesaid, videl't, the fyfte yere of Kyng Edward the Sixte.

> By me JOHN TREVELYAN.   Per me BARTH'M COMBE.
> ℙ me HUGONEM HYLLE.
> L.S.   L.S.   L.S.

[At the back as follows:]

Sealyd and delyveryd the daye and yeare within mencyonyd at Canyngton, in the Countye of Som^t, in the presence of Robert Molynes of Brygewater, yn the seyd Com. of Som., and John Cosin of Langworth, Gent.

WILL OF JOHN TREVELYAN OF YERNSCOMBE.[a]

In the name of God, amen. The seven and twentie daye of Januarie, in the yeare of our Lord God a thowsande fyve hundrith fortie and fyve, I, John Trevelyan, esquyar, of the parishe of Yernescombe, whole in mynd, and of good remembrance, make my testament and last will in fowrme and maner folowinge: Fyrst, I bequeth my Sowlle unto Almighti God, and my bodie to be buried in holie grave accordinge to the discrecion of myne Executors. Item, I geave and bequethe to the Sead store of the parrish church of Yernescombe ten shillingis. Item, I geave and bequethe to everie of my dowghters, that is to saye, fyrste, to Jone my dowghter, alredie maried, Two Hundrethe markis sterlinge. Item, unto Isabell my dowghter, towardes hir mariage, Two Hundrithe markys sterlinge. Item, unto my dowghter Dorothie, towardes hir mariage, Two Hundrethe markys sterlinge: under this condicion, that they marie by the good advice and cowncell of Avice my wiffe and John Trevylyan my sonne and heyre. Which Sixe hundrithe markys I wolde will to be paide by my wiffe Avice and John Trevilyan my sonne and heyre, at such convenient tyme and speade after my decease as they shall thinke best, be equall porcyons. Whyche Avice and John I ordeyne and make my whole and sole executors to se thes my Legacis and bequestes trewlie paid and performyd, and all my debtis lykewise and other chargis that shalbe bestowed at my funerall and obytt according to ther discrecion. The residue of my gooddes not bequethed I bequeth and geave wholie to the forenamyd Avice and John, to order it for the welthes of my sowll according to ther discrecyon. In wytnes wherof I have cawsyd this testament to be made and writen the daie and yeare

---

[a] The indorsement of this Probate merely is as follows : " *Ult. Volunt. Johannis Trevylyan, ar. sen.* 1558; " but the will itself bears date in 1545, and is subscribed only by the witness " Symon Atkyn, clerke."

above specyfyd, berynge wytnes to the same Symon Atkyn, clerke, and George Pollerde.

Probatum fuit pred. testamentum coram nobis Roberto Fysher, &c. Quinto die mensis Maij Anno Domini miſto quingen^mo Quinquage^mo Octavo, &c.

PARDON TO THOMAS BONEVILE.*

HENRICUS dei grã Rex Anglie Francie et Dominus Hiꝺnie oñibus Ballivis et fidelibȝ suis ad quos p̄ntes ꝉre ꝑvenerint salꞇm. Sciatis q̄d de grã nr̃a sꝑali et ex certa scientia et mero motu nr̃is ꝑdonavim⁹ remisim⁹ et relaxavim⁹ Thome Bonevile de Northlegh in coñ Cornuꝺ Armiꝗo seu quocumq alio noĩe censeaꞇ oñimodos t⸗nsgressiones offensas mesprisiones contemptus et impeticõoes ꝑ ip̄m Thomam ante nonũ diem Aprilis ultimo p̄ꝉitum cont⸗ formam statutoꝛ de liꝺatis pannoꝛ et capicioꝛ ſc̄os sive ꝑpetratos unde punicio caderet in finem et redempc̃õem aut in alias penas pecuniarias seu imprisonamenta statutis p̄dc̄is non obstantibȝ Et insuꝑ ex motu et scientia nr̃is p̄dc̄is ꝑdonavim⁹ remisim⁹ et relaxavim⁹ eidem Thome sectam pacis nr̃e que ad nos ꝟsus ip̄m ꝑtinet ꝑ oñimodis ꝑdicõoibȝ murdris raptibȝ mulieꝛ rebellionibȝ insurreccõoibȝ feloniis conspiracõoibȝ cambipartiis manutenciis et imbraciariis ac aliis t⸗nsgressionibȝ offensis negligenciis extorcõoibȝ mesprisionibȝ ignoranciis contemptibȝ concelamentis forisſc̄uris et decepcõoibȝ ꝑ ip̄m Thomam ante dc̄m nonũ diem Aprilis qualiꝑcumq ſc̄is sive ꝑpetratis. Aceciam utlagaꝛ si que in ip̄m Thomam hiis occõonibȝ seu eaꝛ aliqua ſꝺint ꝑmul-

---

* Thomas Bonevile or Bonville was probably a relative of William Lord Bonville, who was beheaded 39 Hen. VI. Perhaps his uncle, a brother of his father John, named in the will of his grandfather Sir William Bonville, made in 1407, and printed in Collectanea Topographica et Genealogica, viii. 244. The same person appears in 1422 as witness to a deed between the Abbot of Newenham, co. Devon, and Alice widow of the above Sir William. Ibid. 216. The pardon is on parchment, with the Great Seal in white wax attached.

gate et firmam pacem nr̃am ei inde concedim⁹. Ita tamen q̃d stet
recto in Cur̃ nr̃a si quis ꝟsus eum loqui voluꝯit de p̃missis vel aliquo
p̃missoꝛ Dumtamen idem Thomas p̃ditor de aliqua p̃dic̃o̅e p̃onam
nr̃am tangente palam vel occulte non existat Et ulꝯius pdonavim⁹
remissim⁹ et relaxavim⁹ eidem Thome om̃imoda escapia felonũ catalla
felonũ et fugitivorũ catalla utlagator̃ et felonũ de se deodanda vasta
impetic̃o̅es ac om̃imodos articulos itin⁹is destruc̃c̃o̅es et t̃ꝰnsgressiones
de viridi vel venac̃o̅e vendic̃o̅em boscor̃ infra forestas et extꝛꝰ et
aliar̃ rer̃ quar̃cumq̃ ante dc̃m nonũ diem Aprilis infra regnũ nr̃m
Ang̃l et March̃ Wallie em̃g̃ et euen̅t unde punicio caderet in
demandam debi̅t seu in finem et redempc̃o̅em aut in alias penas
pecuniarias seu in forisfc̃uram bonor̃ et catallor̃ aut imprisonamenta
seu am̃ciamenta co̅itatum villar̃ vel singulariũ p̃onar̃ vel in on⁹a-
c̃o̅em libe teñ eor̃ qui numq̃ꝰm t̃ꝰnsgressi fuerunt ut heredum exe-
cutor̃ vel ꝑre tenenciũ Escaetor̃ Vicecomitum Coronator̃ et alior̃
hujusmodi et om̃e id quod ad nos ꝟsus ip̃m Thomam ptinet seu
ptinere posset ex causis supꝛ dc̃is. Aceciam pdonaverimus remisim⁹ et relaxavi⁹ eidem Thome om̃imodas donac̃o̅es alienac̃o̅es et
pquisic̃o̅es p ip̃m de ꝑris et teñ de nob vel ꝑgenitorib; nr̃is
quondam Regib; Ang̃l in capite tentis. Aceciam om̃imodas donac̃o̅es
et pquisic̃o̅es ad manũ mortuam fc̃as et h̃itas absq̃ licencia Regia
necnon om̃imodos intrusiones et ingressus in hereditatem suam in
parte vel in toto post mortem antecessor̃ suor̃ absq̃ debita p̃ecuc̃o̅e
ejusdem extꝛꝰ manũ Regiam ante eundem nonũ diem Aprilis fac̃t
una cum exitib; et ꝑficuis inde medio tempore pceptis. Et insuꝑ
pdonavim⁹ remisim⁹ et relaxavim⁹ eidem Thome om̃imodas penas ante
dc̃m nonũ diem Aprilis forisfc̃as coram nob seu consilio nr̃o can-
cellario Thes̃ seu aliquo Judicum nr̃or̃ p aliqua causa et om̃es alias
penas tam nob q̃ꝰm carissimo pr̃i nr̃o defuncto p ip̃m Thomam p
aliqua causa ante eundem nonũ diem Aprilis forisfc̃as et ad opus
nr̃m levan̅d ac om̃imodas securitates pacis ante eundem nonũ
diem Aprilis similiꝯ forisfc̃as. Aceciam t̃cias pciar̃tcias om̃imodor̃
prisonarior̃ in guerra captor̃ nob dc̃o nono die Aprilis qualiꝯcumq̃
debitas ptinentes seu spectantes p eundem Thomam necnon om̃imo-

does t̄nsgressiones offensas mesprisiones contemptus et impeticões p
ip̄m Thomam ante eundem nonū diem Aprilis cont̄ formam tam
quoȓcumq̇ statutoȓ ordinacionū et pvisionū ante dc̄m nonū diem
Aprilis ffoȓ sive editoȓ de pquisicõibȝ acceptacõibȝ leccõibȝ publica-
cõonibȝ notificacõibȝ et execucõibȝ quibuscumq̇ quarumcumq̇ t̄raȓ
et bullaȓ apticaȓ ante dc̄m nonū diem Aprilis et oīm alioȓ statutoȓ
ordinacionū et pvisionū p̄textu quoȓ aliqua secta v̄sus eundem Thomam
p billam vel p brē de p̄muniri fac̄ seu alio modo quocumq̇ p aliqua
mat̄ia ante eundem diem Aprilis fieri valeat q̇m quoȓcumq̇ alioȓ
statutoȓ fc̄os sive ppetratos statutis ordinacõonibȝ et pvisionibȝ illis non
obstantibȝ. Aceciam pdonavim⁹ remisim⁹ et relaxavim⁹ eidem Thome
om̄imod̄ fines adjudicatos am̄ciamenta exitus forisfc̄os relevia scuta-
gia ac om̄imoda debita compota p̄stita arreragia firmaȓ et compotoȓ
nob̄ ante primū diem Septembȓ anno regni nȓi vicesimo qualit̄cumq̇
debita et ptiū necnon om̄imodas accões et demandas quas nos solus
vel nos conjunctim cum aliis psonis vel alia psona hemus seu here
pot̄im⁹ v̄sus ipm̄ Thomam p̄ aliquibȝ hujusmodi finibȝ am̄ciamentis
exitibȝ releviis scutagiis debitis compotis p̄stitis et arreragiis ante
eundem primū diem Septembȓ nob̄ debitis. Aceciam utlagaȓ in ipm̄
Thomam pmulgatas p aliqua causaȓ sup̄dc̄aȓ om̄imodis debitis et
compotis nob̄ debitis et ptinentibus que vigore t̄raȓ nȓaȓ patenciū seu
brīum nȓoȓ de magno vel privato sigillo aut p estallamenta sive
assignacões respectuata existunt omīno exceptis. Ita q̇d p̄sens pdonacio nȓa quo ad p̄missa seu aliquod p̄missoȓ non cedat in dampnū
p̄judiciū vel derogacõem alicujus alt̄ius psone q̇m psone nȓe dum-
taxat proviso semp q̇d nulla hujusmodi pdonacio nȓa aliquo modo
valeat allocet̄ nec fiat nec aliqualit̄ se extendat ad Alianoram
Cobeham filiam Reginaldi Cobeham militis Joh̄em Bolton de Bolton
in Com̄ Lanc̄ Bladsmyth Willm Wyghale nup custodem gaole nȓe
de Notyngham nec ad eoȓ aliquem neq̇ ad feloniam de morte Cris-
tofori Talbot militis felonice inf̄ecti nup ppetratam nec q̇d p̄sens
pdonacio nȓa nec aliqua hujusmodi pdonacio nȓa aliqualit̄ se extendat
quo ad aliquas lanas seu pelles lanutas seu alias m̄candisas de stapula
ad aliquas partes ext̄as ext̄ regnū nȓm Angt̄ cont̄ formam statuti

in parliamento nr̃o apud Westm̃ in crastino sc̃i Martini anno regni
nr̃i decimo octavo tento editi seu aliquor̃ alior̃ statutor̃ cariatas et
traductas nec ad aliquas forisfc̄uras nob̃ debitas in hac parte ptinentes
sive spectantes nec ad exon⁹ ac̃ones sive acquietac̃ões aliquar̃ psonar̃
de punic̃õib3 sup ip̃as fiend juxta formam eor̃dem statutor̃ p aliquib3
lanis sive pellibus lanutis vel aliis m̃candisis de stapula ad aliquas
hujusmodi partes exl̃as cont⁴⁴ formam eor̃dem statuor̃ cariatis sive
traductis Nec q̃d p̃sens pdonacio nr̃a nec aliqua hujusmodi pdonacio
nr̃a ad aliquos magnos computantes nr̃os videl̃t ad Thesaurarios
Cales̃ et hospicii nr̃i vitellarios Cales̃ Camerarios Cestr̃ Northwal̃t et
Suthwal̃t Custodes Garderobe hospicii nr̃i aut Custodes magne
Garderobe nr̃e aut custodes sive cl̃icos Garderobe nr̃e cl̃icos opacionũ
nr̃ar̃ Constabularios Burdegal̃t Thesaurarios l̃re nr̃e Hib̃nie Recep-
tores Ducatus nr̃i Lancastr̃ et ducatus nr̃i Cornub̃ tam gen⁹ales
q⁴⁴m pticulares quo ad aliqua hujusmodi occupac̃ões suas aut alicujus
eor̃dem tangencia ullo modo se extendat. In cujus rei testimoniũ
has l̃ras ñras fieri fecim⁹ patentes. Teste me ip̃o apud Westm̃ vicesimo die Marcii anno regni nr̃i vicesimo quinto.

p ip̃m Regem in parliamento.

PEMBERTON.

---

79.   ADMISSION OF JOHN PAMPYNG TO THE PRIVILEGES OF THE
BROTHERS MINORS OF WINCHESTER.ᵃ

In Xr̃o sibi kĩmo Johanni P̃apyng frat̃ Joh̃nes fr̃m mĩo3 Wintonie gardian⁹ l̃ su⁹ salutẽ l̃ p piẽtis vite merita regna celestia pro-
mereri Cũ sc̃issim⁹ in Xr̃o pat̃ l̃ Dñs dñs Sixt⁹ diviã providencia
papa quart⁹ nõ solũ fr̃b3 l̃ sororib3 nr̃i ordĩs set eciã 9fr̃ib3 l̃ 9sororib3

ᵃ The original is on parchment, with a fragment of the monastic seal in red and green
wax, attached by a silken cord of red and green threads. The name and date of month
are in a different hand from the rest of the document, of which a number were probably
kept in store for use as occasion might require.

eiusdem lr̄as suffragiales habentibȝ de bn̄ignitate aptica ḡrose conces-
serit qᵈ q'libȝ eoȝ possit sibi elig̃e idoneū ꝯfessorẽ q̄ ip̄os ꝉ ip̄oȝ q̄libet
ab oībȝ ꝉ singulis om̄ibȝ excessibȝ et p̄atis, in sin͠glis sedi ap̄licæ refvatis
casibȝ semel dūtaxat hoc anno a publicac̃õe ɫraȝ papaɫm ꝯputando
vidȝ a quarto die mens̃ ap̄lis, ꝉ semel in mortis artĩclo, ab aliis vero
tociens quociens opus foret, absolv͠e ꝉ penā salutarẽ indḡe posset,
idemq̄ vel alius ꝯfessor plenariã oīm p̃ctoȝ eoȝdem remissionẽ in
vero mortis artĩclo valeret elargiri p lr̄as suas ap̄licas benigne in-
dulceit. Idcirco vr̄e devoc̃õis q̄ ob Xr̄i revenciã ad nr̄am habetis
ordinẽ sincerū cõsiderans aff c̃m̄ ꝉ acceptans vos in nr̄am ꝯfraɫatẽ ꝉ ad
uniṽa ꝉ sin͠gla fr̄m admīst͔ c̃õnȝ anglicane suffragia recipio tenore
p̄ncum̄ in vita put ꝉ in morte ut dictis aplicis p̄vilegiis om̄nqȝ bonoȝ
sp̄ualm̄ bn̄ficiis scd̃m formā ꝉ eff c̃m̄ eoȝdẽ pfruam̄ vr̄e aīe ad salutem,
rediciens nichilomin⁹ de gr̄a sp̄ali ut cū post obitū vr̄m pv̄ẽn̄ sc̃a
fuerit exhibic̃õ ɫraȝ in nr̄o p̄vciali capɫo eadem pro vobis fiet rec̃õ-
mendac̃õ q̄ p fr̄ibȝ nr̄is defunctis ibidem c̃õiter fieri ꝯsuevit. Valete
in Xr̄o ihu ꝉ orate p me. Daɫ Wintonie q͛rto die mens̃ Marcii Anno
Dn̄i Miɫɫmo ccocᵐᵒlxxixⁿᵒ.

INDULGENCE GRANTED BY JOHANNES DE GIGLIIS TO JOHN PAMPYNG.ᵃ

Johannes de Gigliis alias de liliis Ap̄ticus Subdiacon⁹ Et in In-
clito Regno Anglie fructuū ꝉ proventuū camere ap̄tice debitoȝ Col-
lector/ Et Perse⁹ de Malviciis decanus Eccɫie Sancti Michael̃ de

---

ᵃ With the exception of the name of the grantee, and date of the month, which are written,
it is printed on parchment, in small sharp black-letter type, probably from a Roman press.
A fragment of the seal in red wax is attached by a strip cut from another copy of the form.
We subjoin the following from Fuller's "Church History," edit. 1655, xv cent. book iv.
" John Giglis, an Italian, about this time employed by the Pope, got an infinite mass of
money, having power from the Pope to absolve people from usury, symonie, theft, man-
slaughter, fornication, adultery, and all crimes whatsoever, saving smiting of the clergie, and
conspiring against the Pope, and some few cases reserved alone to His Holiness : This

leproseto Bononieñ Sanctissimi domini nostri pape Cubicularius sedis
apostolice Nuntii et commissarii per eundem sanctissimum dominum
nostrum papam ad infra scripta deputati In p̄dicto anglie regno /
Universis presentes litteras Inspecturis Salutem ⁊ sinceram in
domino caritatem /   Noveritis q̃ sanctissimus in cristo pater ⁊ dñs
ñr p̄fatus Nobis Johãni ⁊ Perseo c̃õmissariis p̄nominatis c̃õcedendi
universis christi fidelib3 In regno Anglie/ ⁊ dominio hybernie Lo-
cisq, ac terris quibuscunq, dicti regni dicioni subiectis qui per se vel
aliũ Infra temp⁹/ ad sc̃issimi dñi nr̄i ⁊ sedis aptice bñplacitũ duratu3
⁊ usquequo eiusdem bñplaciti revocacio aut 9tento3 in suis literis
suspensis facta fuerit sc̃m tenorẽ ipsa3 litera3 aptica3/ Qui ad
ipugnandũ infideles ⁊ resistendũ eo3 conatib3/ Tantũ Quatuor
Tres vel Duos vel unũ florenos auri Vel tm̄ qñtum per nos Cõmissarios
prefatos desuper deputatos/ seu cũ collectorib3 a nobis super hoc 9sti-
tuendis vel facultatẽ hñtibus convenerint/ ⁊ cũ effectu persolverint/
Ut Confessor ydone⁹ presbiter secularis vel cuiusvis ordinis etiã
mendicantiũ Regularis curat⁹ vel non curat⁹/ quẽ quilibet eo3
duxerit eligendũ/ eligẽtis ⁊ eligentiùm cõfessione audita seu cõfes-
fessionib3 respective auditis pro cõmissis per eũ vel eos peccatis
criminib3 ⁊ excessib3 quibuscunq, qñtũcumq, enormib3 ⁊ gravib3 /
eciã si talia forẽt propter que sedes aptica eẽt quovismodo cõsulenda/
Cõspirac̃õis In romanũ Pontificẽ ⁊ in predictam sedem apticam/ ⁊
iniectionis manuũ violẽta3 In Ep̄os et superiores prelatos crimĩbus
dũtaxat exceptis Necnõ a censuris ⁊ penis eccłiasticis quibuscũq,
quomõcunq, inflictis a Jure vel ab hoĩe semel in vita ⁊ in aliis dicte
sedi nõ reservatis casib3 ⁊ peccatis quociẽs id pecierint eis auctoritate
Aplica de absolucionis bñficio providere ⁊ tam semel in vita q̃ in

Giglies got for himself the rich bishoprick of Worcester; yea, we observe, that in that see
a team of four Italians followed each other:

    1. John Giglis.   3. Julius de Medicis, afterwards Clement the 7th.
    2. Silvester Giglis.   4. Hieronymus de Negutiis.

Thus, as weeds in a garden, once got in, hardly got out, as sowing themselves, so these
Italians, having planted themselves in that rich place, were never gotten out (pleading as
it were prescription of almost forty years' possession) till the power of the Pope was partly
banished England, and then Hugh Latimer was placed in the bishoprick."

mortis articulo plenariã oĩm suoӡ pc̄toӡ remissionem ꝉ absolucioēӡ cū ea plenaria Indulgencia quã eciã assequerentur In visitacione liminū Beatoӡ apꝉoӡ Petri ꝉ Pauli/ ꝉ Basilicaӡ sancti Johãnis late- ranen̄ Et beate Marie maioris de urbe ac recuperacione terre sancte eorūdem infidelium expugnacĭŏe / ac Anno Jubileo que eciã ad p̄ctã oblita ꝉ que alias aliis sacerdotibus cōfessi forēt extendaꝉ Ipsis in sīceritate fidei ꝉ unitate sc̄e Romane ecc̄ie ac obediēcia ꝉ devocione sc̄issimi dn̄i nostri ꝉ successoӡ suoӡ Romanoӡ Pontificū Canonice intrācium persistentibӡ impendere ꝉ salutarē penitēciã iniungere Ita ut si ipsis in hm̃oi mortis articulo sepius cōstitutis absolucio ipsa impen- daꝉ / Nichilomin⁹ iterato in vero mortis articulo possit impendi ꝉ im- pēss suffragetur eisdē auctoritate apꝉica de apꝉice potestatis plenitudine concessit facultatem prout in ipsis litteris apꝉicis super hoc emanatis plenius continetur Cū auꝉ JOHANNES PAMPYNG Infra prefatū tēpus dicti beneplaciti de facultatibӡ suis competentem quãtitatem ad opus fidei h̃mõi ac ad expugnacionem Infidelium Contulerit / Idcirco tenore presentium h̃mõi Confessoris eligendi eis Auctoritate apostu- lica qua In hac parte fungimur satisfacto tamen hiis quibus fuerit satisfaccio impendenda plenam ac liberam tribuim⁹ facultatem / Datum sub sigillo Sancte Cruciate Anno Incarnacionis Dn̄ice Mil- lesimo Quadringētesimo Nono Dicꞇ tercio die Mensis Marcii.

PETITION FROM SIR JOHN TREVELYAN TO THE KING.[a]

A.D. 1

Petition from Sir John Trevylian, Knight, to be heard before the King as to his title to certain Manors in Glamorganshire, of which he had been wrongfully dispossessed.

TO THE KYNGE OUR SOVERAYNE LORDE.

Umbely sheweth unto your most nobill grace your faithefull ser- vaunt and true liegeman John Trevylian, Knyght, that, where your

[a] In Part I. pp. 81, 82 of "The Trevelyan Papers" are inserted two documents from an ancient parchment volume belonging to the Trevelyan family. The two documents

said orator was seased in fee of the mannors of Michelstowe, Wrencheston, and Lancarvan, with ther appurtenances, in your Countie of Glamorgan in Wales, of the wiche premisses your said orator in the life of Jasper your nobill uncle late Duke of Bedford was pesseably seassed, at wiche tyme Water Herberd, Knyght, nowe decessed, so because the said mannors lay and were nye adioynyng unto hym, by dyverse meanys labored and desired of the said Sr John to by his interese and take in the premisses, and for because he coulde not atteyne his purpose in the premisses of the said Sr John, the said Sir Water of his grete might and power by colour feyned a title to the said mannors, and into the same, withoute any title of right, ayenst your lawes, entredde, and the same with grete myght wrongefully occupied the possession by longe season, whiche mannors my ladye Anne, late wiff to the said Sr Water, nowe hathe and occupieth withoute any title of right, contrarie to your lawes, wiche said ladye is in thos parties of so grete myght and power, and also soe gretely kynned and alied of blode by the reason of Edward Duke of Buckyngham her brother, that your said orator in no wise canne prevaile to sue for his right accordyng to his title in the premisses after the dewe cours of your lawes in your said Countie. Plesith hit therfore your highnes of your most habundante grace to graunt your graciouse letters missive to be directid to the same said ladye Anne, commandyng her by the same to brynge in by her councell before your highnes, or your most discrete councell, at the quindesme of Seynt Hillarie nex comyng, wheresoever your Grace shalbe, all evydencis that she hath concernyng her title in the premisses; and ther to stonde and obbey suche order and direccion as shalbe ordred and made by your highnes and your said Councell in this behalffe. And your said orator shall dayly pray unto Godde for the prosperus preservacion of your nobill estate longe to endure.

<hr>

which we now print apparently relate to the same matter at a somewhat subsequent date. They are both on parchment, and both without day or month. See also Collect. Top. et Geneal. ii, p. 391.

RELEASE FROM THE DUKE OF SUFFOLK TO JOHN TREVELYAN A.D. 14
OF LANDS IN WALES.[a]

Omnibus X̄p̄i fidelibus ad quos presens scriptum pervenerit nos
Johes Dux Suffolch Consanguineus et heres Thome Chaucers
armigeri salutem in Dño sempiternam   Cum Johes Trevilian armig̃
p̃ corpore dni Regis est consanguineus et heres Simonis Ralegh
armigeri et Johis Ralegh militis videlicet filius Elizabethe nuper
uxoris Johis Trevilian armigeri filie Thome Walesburgh armigeri
filii Johe Walesburgh sororis dicti Simonis et filie dicti Johis
Ralegh militis ac Ricardus Trevilian existent in plena et pacifica
possessione ad presens in maneriis de Michelstow, Wringeston, Lancarvan et Lantwit cum suis ptiñ una cum advocacione Ecclesie de
Michelstow predict̃ necnon in reddit̃ et serviciis tam liberorum quam
villanorum dictis maneriis et utriusque eorum pertinent̃ sive spec-
tant̃ cum eorum sect̃ et sequel̃ tam procreatis quam procreand̃ necnon
in omnibus meis terris teñ reddit̃ revers̃ et servic̃ cum suis ptiñ
que nuper fuerunt dictorum Simonis Ralegh et Johannis Ralegh in
Wallia infra com̃ Glomargan et Morgannok sicut habemus ex cog-
nicione et relacione virorum fide dignorum.   Nos igitur considera-

---

[a] In the original from which our copy is taken there is a label for the seal, and blanks
are left for the date of the day and month, but the year of the king's reign is given. The
Duke of Suffolk was John de la Pole, son of William Duke of Suffolk and Alice daughter and heir of Sir Thomas Chaucer. John was married to Elizabeth, second daughter
of Richard Duke of York, and was consequently brother (in law) to Edward IV. as
designated in the letter to him from that king written in favour of the claim of John
Trevelyan, and already printed by this Society in Trevelyan Papers, Pt. I. p. 82. T
these we may add the subsequent document, likewise on parchment, and derived, like
the other documents, from the family records :—

" The reioinder of John Trevilian, Knyght, to the reioinder of the Lady Anne. The
seid John Trevilian seith and verryfyith yn ev'y thyng as he yn hys seid bylle and replica-
c'on hath seid, w'oute that the moder of the seid Duke of Suff' died seised of the seid
mannors, londs, and tenements, or of eny p'te therof, or that hys seid moder was att en y
tyme seased of the seid mannors, londs, and tenements, or of eny p'te therof, yn hyr
demene, as of fee or of eny other state of enheritaunce, as in hyr seid reioinder is surmysed.
All whyche matters he is redy to veryfye and prove.''

cione premissa et certis aliis causis nos moventibus remississe, relax-
asse et omnino pro nobis et heredibus nostris quietum clamasse pre-
fatis Johanni Trevilian et Ricardo Trevilian et heredibus ipsius
Johannis Trevilian imperpetuum totum ius nostrum et clam̄ iuris
que umquam habuimus habemus seu in futurum habere potuimus de
et in dictis maneriis de Michelstow, Wrengeston, Lancarvan et Lantwit, una cum advocacione Ecclesie predicte de Michelstow, cum
omnibus et singulis suis pertiñ necnon in reddit̄ et servic̄ tam
liberorum tenencium quam villanorum dictis maneriis et eorum
utriusque pertinent̄ suis spectantibus cum eorum sectis et sequelis
tam pereat̄ quam pereand̄ necnon de et in omnibus meis terris teñ
reddit̄ revers̄ et serviciis cum suis ptinent̄ que nuper fuerunt predicti Simonis Ralegh et predicti Joħis Ralegh militis in Wallia infra
comit̄ predictis.   Ita quod nec nos prefat̄ Dux nec heredes nostri
nec aliquis alius nomine iuris sive titulo nostris aliquod ius titulum
seu clam̄ iuris in p̄dictis maneriis cum advocatione predict̄ et suis
pertın necnon in reddit̄ et serv̄ tam liberorum tenencium quam
villanorum dictis maneriis et eorum utriusque pertinent̄ sive spec-
tant̄ cum eorum sectis et sequelis tam procreatis quam procreandis,
necnon de et in omnibus meis terris reddit̄ revers̄ et servic cum
pertiñ suis que nuper fuerunt dc̄i Simonis Ralegh et dc̄i Johannis
Ralegh et eorum cuj'libet in Wallia infra comit̄ predictos de cetero
exigere clamare seu vendicare potuimus seu debemus in futurum et
ab omni accione iuris sumus exclusi inperpetuum per present̄.   In
cuius rei testimonium huic presenti scripto nostro sigillum nostrum
apposuimus et signo nostro manual̄ assignavimus.   Hiis testibus,
Edmundo Mountford milite, Edmundo Hambden armigero p corpore d̄ni Regis, Joħe Boteler, Matheo Cradok armigero, Mauricio
Botcler gentelman et aliis.

Dat̄   die Mens̄   Anno regni Regis Henrici
septimi post conq̄um Anglie tercio.

Hiesus. Maria.

Be hit remembyrd That the xix yere off kynge Harry the viijth
and in the xviijth day off January then preseynt: the withyn namyd
John Cavell, Gentleman, and Richard Howell, yeman, came unto
the mannor off Whalesborowh nygh unto Stratton in the cownty off
Cornwall, and there the forseid Richard by the vertew and aucto-
rite off the letter off Attorney heere within wrytten, gave livery
and possession unto the seid John Cavell off three closes there,
wheroff the ffyrst is callid Wydmauth or the Mayn, the second
Chappell Close or the Chappell parke, the thyrd Myddylhill or Myd-
derhyll, to the same intent, purpoose, and effect as in certeyn Inden-
tors maade bytween the withyn namyd John Trevillyan and Gyles
Hyll Esqwyers, berynge date the xxiiijth day off September and the
xvijth yere off the seid kynge Harry the viijth, moore playnly is ex-
pressid.   Thes Men there then beinge present and lawfully re-
qwyred to record the same: That is to weet, Willm. Acheeffe otherwyse called Willm. Stanbery, Richard Lamerton, Petyr Farr, Thomas
Synggar, John Greyston, John Twygges, John Richard, Robt. Glan-
vild, Robt. Gosse, Robt. Sawnders, Watyr Ley, John Poope, Robt.
Walky, Willm. Dodgall, and others.

Att Whallesborowh affore seid, the yere, day, and moneth above
writton.

LORD CHIEF JUSTICE JOHN FITZ JAMES TO MR. CRUMWELL.[b] A. D.

Jhs.

Master Crumwell. After most hartie recommendation, with like
thankes for your manyfold kyndenes. Thys is to advertise yow of

---

[a] The original Letter of Attorney is dated 21 Oct. 19 Hen. VIII. and what follows is
indorsed upon it.

[b] From the original, entirely in the handwriting of the Chief Justice, preserved in the
State Paper Office. It was not usual at that period to give the date of the year, but it was

the resceit of your gentill letter send me by the servaunt of Mr. Trevelyan, whiche hade resceyvede a Privey Seale apon payn of allegeaunce, before the comynge of your letter to me, and was yn his journey toward London, so that iffe his fortune be goode, he may kepe his apparaunce; hartily praying yow to be gode master to hym. Trew it ys there is moche labour made ageyn hym by mean of the wiffe of a gentleman yn thies parties callide Mr. Hill, whos doffter is maryed to the son of the saide Trevelyan; wherfore sche wold bynd hym to certen thynges other than be compriside yn ther indenture of mariage, wherof sche hathe nor wretynge ne yet proffe; but the verie trouthe this Trevelian is not the wyseste man, ne yett of a seurtie no ydeott, but a man off litill discretion, and not broken, but hath allwey lyved at home withowte any brekyng. And bycause he wold not folowe the mynd off the gentlewoman sche hathe made this labour ageyn hym, more as I suppose to prove hym a ydeotte than for eny truste of her bargeyn. Iff he be a ydeotte, on my feythe I wold the Kyngges Heighnes hade righte of hym. How be it, seurly iffe he be examined accordyng to the Statute he will not be provide ydeote, as yn that mater ye knowe what ye have to do, and so do I iffe I were with yow. But for the resideu of the mater I hartely pray yow do as ye have written and he schall seurly deserve your payn. As to my self, I am the moste unhappie creature lyvyng, that syns my Soverayn Lord wold have me to do hym servyce, that by reason of this unhappie ynfirmytie I kan not be able to cum to the place wher I schueld do hym servyce. For by the feythe I owe to God and to his Grace, how be it I am moste unable to do His Grace servyce of any of his Justices, yett iff I were able to labour I wold seurly, God willyng, bee among yow, and do the best I kowde; but, by the othe I have made byfore, I am not able to take suche a journey withowte moche perill off my

probably 1533, before Crumwell became Secretary to the King. Mr. Trevelyan was John, who married Avice Cockworthy; he died in 1546 ; his son John, born in 1508, married Maud, daughter of Gyles Hyll and Agatha Brent: a pedigree of this family of Hyll is given in Collectanea Topog. et Geneal. vol. i. p. 409.

life. And if I were ther yett I kowde not goo withowte a staff, so that the absens fro my Soverayn Lord at this tyme grevithe me more than my ynfirmite. And yett on my feythe dyvers tymes in my sikenes I wold have yeven all the litill gode I have to have bene easide off my payn. Gentill Master Crumwell, now I have made yow my gostely fader yn this mater, more specially than I have wreten to eny man lyvynge, hartely praying you to make my excusse to my Soverayn Lord, as ye shall see tyme. And I schall dayly pray for His Grace, and iffe I die and never cum at London, yet I schall so deserve parte of your payn that ye shall be content by Goddes mercy, who preserve you.

At my poor howse the 8th day of Marche [1533].

Your own assuride,
JOHN FITZJAMES.

THE PILGRIMAGE OF GRACE. PETITION OF WALTER COURTENEY A. D. 1 TO THE KING FOR CERTAIN MANORS.[a]

To the King our liege Lord.

In most humble wyse sheweth unto your highness your trew and feithfull subjett and liegeman Water Courteney knyght, that when he beyng in your service in the parties of Brytaign and Fraunce

<hr>

[a] What was called " The Pilgrimage of Grace " occurred in 1536, and assumed the character of a rebellion : in it John Lord Scrope was implicated, and from the above document it appears that he had committed some ravages upon the property of Walter Courteney, in Devonshire, the latter being nearly related, if not brother, to Henry Courteney, Marquis of Exeter, and to Peter Courteney, Bishop of that diocese. Walter Courteney appealed to the King, set forth his losses by Scrope and his "affinity," and claimed certain manors in Essex and Devonshire to re-imburse him. We may perhaps presume that the parties to whom the manors belonged, and who are named in the instrument, were of the "affinity" of John Lord Scrope. See Stowe's Chron. edit. 1615, p. 967, and Lord Herbert of Cherbury's Henry VIII., in Kennet, vol. ii. p. 207. The original is on parchment.

had his goodis and catellis within your Countie of Devonshire
despoyled and taken away by John Lord Scrope of Bolton and
other of his affinite to the great losse and extreme hurte of the seide
Water without your especiall grace to hym shewed in that behalf,
wherefore please it your highnes, the premises considered, and that
the seid Water is and all tymes hath bene your trew and feithfull
subjett and liege man and soo shall endevour hym self to your
pleasur unto the uttermost of his power, to graunt unto the seid
Water your gracious lettres patentes in dewe forme to be made after
the tenure ensuyng, and he shall pray unto Almyghty God for the
prosperous preservacion of your most Royall estate.

Rex omnibus ad quos, &c. salutem. Sciatis quod nos de gracia
nostra speciali ac consideracione boni et gratuiti servicii quod dilectus
et fidelis serviens noster Walterus Courteney miles nobis impendit
et ante hec tempora tam in partibus transmarinis quam in regno
nostro Angliæ impendebat et indies impendere non desistit, dedimus
et concessimus eidem Waltero Manerium de Nyssal cum suis pertiñ
in cõm Essex quod nuper fuit Johannis le Scrope militis nuper dicť
Dominus le Scrope de Bolton et quod ad manus nostras per forisfactuř eiusdem Johannis le Scrope deven⁹it: ac manerium de Fenyton
cum suis pertiñ in cõm Devoñ ac omnia maneria, messuag̃, terř, teñ,
reversiones, serviĉ, et hereditamenta quecumque que fuerunt Riĉi Mal-
herbe aut alicujus alterius ad eius usum in dicť cõm Devoñ et quæ ad
manus nřas p̃ forisfactuř eiusdem Riĉi devenerunt: ac omnia illa mes-
suag̃, terř, teñ, et hereditameñ quecum₃ infra Civitatem Exoñ in cõm
Devoñ, que nuꝑ fueř Johis att Well aut alicuius alterius ad eius
usum in dicť civitate, et que ad manus nostras per forisfactuř eiusdem Johis att Well deveneř; necnon maneř de Coryton cum suis
ptineñ in cõm Devoñ ac maneria de Newcton et Trancreke cum
ptiñ in cõm Cornub que quidem maneria nuper fueř Johis Coryton;
ac eciam omnia illa maneria, messuag̃, terř, tẽnta, et hereditamenta
quecumq₃ que fueř eiusdem Johis aut alicuius alterius ad eius usum
in dicť cõm Devoñ et Cornub que omnia et singula maneria ac
cetera p̃missa p̃fať Johi Coryton ptineñ ad manus nřas p̃ forisfacturam

eiusdem Joħis nup deveneℸ: ħend et tenend maneria p̄dicta ac omnia et singula alia p̄missa ac p̱tiñ una cum feod miliℸ advocaċõibȝ ecclesiaȝ, cantaℸ, p̄bendaȝ et alioȝ beneficioȝ ecclesiasticoȝ quorum-cumq̧, ac cum curiis letis, feriis hundℸ, parcis, warenis et aliis lib⁹tatibȝ, frances, p̱ficiis, rebus et commoditatibȝ quibuscumq̧ eisdem maneriis, terℸ, teñ et ceℙis p̄missis et eoȝ cuiℸt seu alicui inde parceℸt qualiter-cumq̧ p̱tineñℸ sive spectanℸ in tam ampla forma p̱ut dicℸ Joħes le Scrope, Ric̃us Malerbe, Joħes att Well et Joħes Coryton seu eoȝ aliquis ℸone p̄missoȝ seu eoȝ alicuius parceℸt ħueℸ seu eoȝ aliquis ħuit et gavisus fuit, præfaℸ Waltero et hℸdȝ de corpore suo excuntibus de nobis et heredibus nostris per servicium militaℸ absque aliquo alio nobis vel hered nostris reddend seu faciend. Eo quod expressa mentio de vero valore annuo seu aliquo alio valore seu certitudine premissorum aut alicuius inde p̱ceℸt vel de aliis donis aut conces-sionibus eidem W. per nos ante hec tempora facta in presenℸ mi-nime existit aut aliquo statuto, actu, ordinacione, p̱visione, seu concessione in contrarium facℸ, ordinaℸ seu p̱viꝫ non obstanℸ.

In cuius, &°. Teste, &ᶜ

MARRIAGES OF TREVELYANS AND CHICHESTERS.[a]

This Indenture made the sixth daie of Maie in the tenth yeare of the raigne of our Soveraigne Ladie Elizabeth, by the Grace of God Quene of Englaund, Fraunce, and Yrlaunde, defendour of the Faith, &c. Betwene John Trevylian of Nettlecomb, in the countie of Somerset, Esquire, of thone parte, and Sir John Chechestre o℈ Raw-

[a] The following is the counterpart executed by Sir John Chichester: the fellow-deed was signed and sealed by John Trevelyan. The date on the indorsement is 10 Eliz. 1568, and it is in this form: "The Covenaunce betwene Sʳ John Chichestre and John Trevelyan of Trevelyan. Agreement between Sir John Chichester, Kt., and John Tre-velyan, Esq. the father, previous to the marriage of John Trevelyan the son with Urith Chichester." We print it with all the old legal formalities and repetitions, then usual in instruments of the kind.

leigh, in the countie of Devon, Knight, of thother parte, Wittenessith that, for dyvers good causes and considerations betwene the said parties concluded and agreed upon, hit is nowe covenaunted, graunted, condiscended, and agreed upon betwene the said parties, and the said John Trevilyan, for him, his heires, and executours, covenanteth, promysseth, agreeth, and graunteth to and with the said Sir John Chechestre, Knight, his heires, executours, and assignes, by theise presentes, that the said John Trevilian shall, before the feast daie of Sainte John the Baptist next ensewinge the date hereof, at the costes and charges in the lawe of the said Sir John Chechestre, Knyght, his heires and executours or assignes, make, assure, and convey, or cause to be made, assured, and conveyed, unto Thomas Luttrell, Roger Pridiaux, William Harris, Esquyers, and Brice Hill, gentleman, and to their heires, or to the survivour or survivours of them, and to his and theire heires or to theires of the survivour of them, such good, perfecte, and sufficient estate or estates, assuraunces or conveaunces in the lawe in fee symple, as shalbe reasonablye devysed or advysed by the said Sir John Chechestre, his heires or assignes, or by his or theire learned counsel in the lawe, of and in the Mannours of Nettlecomb, Rowden, Wood Advente, Aller Butler, Olde Knoll, and Venyford, togeather with thadvowson, rectorie, and patronage of the Churche of Nettle-comh, with all and singuler their rightes, members, and appur-tenaunces, and of and in all the messuages, howses, milles, landes, tenements, rents, reversions, services, woodes, underwoodes, waters, fishinges, pastures, medowes, liberties, rectories, advowsons, fraun-chises, and hereditamentes of the said John Trevilyan, with all and singuler their rightes, membres, and appurtenaunces thereunto be-longinge or apperteyninge, set, lyenge, and beinge in Nettle-comb, Rowden, Wood Advent, Aller Butler, Old Knoll, Veny-ford, Stokegomer, Redchuisshe otherwise called Rodhuisshe, Cow-bridge, Styntwill, Hinche, Torchelynche, Dunster, Overholte, West Harewood, and Tymbercomb, in the said countie of Somerset, and of and in all the mannours of Berynarber and Lyttleham, with all and singuler their rightes, membres, and appurtenaunces, and of and in all messuages, howses, landes, tenementes, rentes, reversions, services, woodes, underwoodes, wastes, waters, fishinges, pastures, meadowes, liberties, rectories, advowsons, patronages, franchises, and hereditamentes of the said John Trevilian, with all and singuler their rightes, members, and appurtenances thereunto belonginge or apperteyning, set, lyenge, and beinge in Berynarber and Littleham, in the countie of Devon; and of and in all the mannours of Whalesborough, Trevilion, Trerose, Mawmon, and Uthenoe, with all and singuler their appurtenaunces, and of and in all the messuages, housses, landes, tenementes, rentes, reversions, services, woodes, waters, fishinges, pastures, medowes, liberties, rectories, advowsons, patronages, francheses, and hereditaments of the said John Trevilyan, with all and singuler their rightes, membres, and appertenaunces thereunto belonginge and apperteyninge, set, lyenge, and beinge in Champnehaies and Wolmerhaies in the countie of Dorset; and of and in all and singuler the messuages, houses, landes, tenementes, rentes, reversions, services, woodes, waters, fishinges, pastures, meadowes, liberties, franchises, advowsons, rectories, patronages, and hereditamentes whatsoever, accepted, reputed, used, occupyed, holden, or demysed, as parte, parcell, or member of the said mannours, or of any of them (except before excepted); and also of and in all and singuler messuages, mylles, landes, tenementes, rentes, reversions, services, woodes, underwoodes, wastes, waters, fishinges, pastures, meadowes, liberties, francheses, and hereditamentes of the said John Trevilyan whatsoever, with all and singuler their appurtenaunces (except before excepted) in the severall counties of Somerset, Devon, Cornewall, and Dorset. Which estate and estates, assuraunce and conveyance so to be had and made, shalbe to the severall uses, intentes, purposes, and behouffes hereafter severally expressed and declared, with such provisoes, lymytations, and conditions, and in such manner and fourme as is hereafter expressed and declared in these present Indentures, and to none other uses, intents, behouffs, provysoes, lymytations, conditions, nor purposes. That is to saie, for and in the sayd mannours of Trerose and Uthnoe with the appurtenaunces, and of and in all and singuler the said messuages, landes, tenementes, rentes, reversions, services, and hereditamentes in Trerose, Uthnoe, and Mawnon forsaid, with all and singular their appurtenaunces, to the use and behouf of the said John Trevilian, Esquire, for terme of his life, without any impechment of wast to be commytted or done in any parte or parcell of the premisses last above mentioned; and after his decesse to the use and behouff of such woman as shalbe wif unto the said John Trevilian at the tyme of his decesse, for and during the terme of her lief naturall; and after her decesse, to the use and behowf of John Trevilian, sonne and heire apparant of the said John Trevilian, Esquire, and of the heires males of his bodie lawfully begotten; and, for default of such issue, to the use and behowffe of the heires of the bodie of the said John Trevilian the father lawfully begotten; and, for default of such issue, to the use of the right heires of Josias Trevilian, one other sonne of the said John Trevilian the father, and of the heires males of his body lawfully begotten; and, for defaulte of such issue, to the use and behouffe of Willm Trevilian, one other sonne of the said John Trevilian the father, and of the heires males of his bodie lawfully begoten; and, for defaulte of such issue, to the use of the right heires of the sayd William Trevylyan for ever. And of and in all and singuler those forsaid messuages, landes, tenementes, and hereditamentes, lying and being in Red-huysshe otherwise Rodhuishe, Cowbridge, Styntvill, Lynche, Torche Lynche, Dunster, Overholt, Westharwood, and Tymbercomb afore-sayd, in the sayd countie of Somerset, being parcell of the sayd mannour of Old Knoll, or elles beinge reputed, knowne, or taken as parte, parcell, or membre of the said mannour of Olde Knoll, to the use and behouffe of one Edward Trevilyan, brother unto the said John Trevilian the father, for the terme of the lief of the said Edward; and, after his decesse, to the use and behouffe of the said

John Trevilian the father for terme of his lief, without impechment of wast; and, after his decease, to the use and behouffe of the said John Trevilian the sonne, and of the heires males of his bodie lawfully begotten; and, for defaulte of such issue, to the use and behouf of the said William Trevylyan, and of the heires males of his bodie lawfully begotten; and, for defaulte of suche issue, to the use and behouffe of the said Josias Trevilian, and of the beires males of his bodie lawfully begotten; and, for defaulte of suche issue, to the use of the beires of the bodie of the said John Trevilian the father lawfully begotten: and, for defaulte of such issue, to the use of the right heires of the said William Trevylyan for ever. And of and in the said mannour of Lyttleham, with thappurtenaunces, and of and in all the said messuages, landes, tenementes, and hereditamentes in Littleham forsaid, to the use and behowf of the said John Trevilian the sonne, and of the heires males of his bodie lawfully begotten; and, for defaulte of such issue, to the use and behouffe of the yonger,* and after his decesse to the use and behouf of the said John Trevilian the father, for terme of his lief, without impechment of wast; and, after his decesse, to the use and behoufe of the said John Trevilian the sonne, and of the beires males of his bodie lawfully begotten; and, in defaulte of such issue, to the use and behouff of the said William Trevilian, and of the beires males of his bodie lawfully begotten; and, for defaulte of suche issue, to the use and behoufe of the said Josias Trevilian, and of the heires males of his bodie lawfully begotten; and, for defaulte of suche issue, to the use of the heires of the bodie of the said John Trevilian the father lawfully begotten; and, for defaulte of such issue, to the use and behouffe of the right heires of the said Wittm Trevilian for ever. And of and in the said mannour of Whalesborough, with the appurtenaunces, and of and in all the said messuages, landes, tenementes, rentes, reversions, services, and hereditamentes in Whalesborough forsaid, to the use and behouffe of the said John Trevilian the father, for and untill suche tyme as the said John Trevilian the sonne, or any other that shalbe sonne

* There seems an omission here, but we follow the original.

and heire apparaunte of the said John Trevilian the father, shall happen to marry, espouse, and take to wief one of the daughters of the said Sir John Chichestre. And, after the said marriage had and solemnized, to the use and behouffe of the said sonne and heire apparaunt that shall so happen to mary the doughter of the said Sir John Chechester, for terme of his life, without impechement of wast; and, after his decesse, to the use and behoufe of the sayd doughter, so to the heire apparaunte to be marryed, for terme of her lyef; and, after her decesse, to the use and behoufe of the heires males of the bodie of the said sonne and heire apparaunte, lawfully begotten; and, for defaulte of suche issue, to the use and behouffe of the heires of the bodie of the said John Trevilian the father, law-fully begotten; and, for defaulte of suche issue, to the use and behouffe of the said William Trevilian and of his heires for ever. And for and in the sayd mannour of Allerbutler, with the appur-tenaunces, and of and in all the said messuages, landes, tenementes and hereditamentes in Allerbutler forsaid, to the use of the said John Trevilian the father for terme of his lyeff, without impeche-ment of waste; and, after his decesse, if the seconde sonne of the said John Trevilian the father, lawfully begotten, at the tyme of his death, be not advaunced or preferred by the said John the father to some leasse of landes or tenementes in possession, then to the use of the said seconde sonne untill suche tyme as some reversion of landes and tenementes graunted unto the said seconde sonne by the said John the father shall happen to falle, or untill such tyme as the said John Trevilian the sonne, or the heires male of the bodie of the said John Trevilian the father, shall, be good and sufficient assuraunce in the lawe, assure and convey unto the said seconde sonne one yearly rente of tenne poundes of lawfull money of Englaunde yerely, goyng fourth of suche landes and tenementes whereof the said John Trevilian, the sonne and the heire male of the bodie of the said John Trevilian the father, shalbe then seased of a perfecte estate in fee symple, without condition or other incoumbrances, to have and perceave (*sic*) the said yerely rente unto the said second sonne of the said John Trevilian the father, until suche tyme as some reversion of landes or tenementes graunted unto the said seconde sonne, by the said John the father, shall happen to falle, with one clause of distres therein to be lymitted and conteyned for nonepayment of the said yerely rente, at such daies and tymes as in the same assuraunce and conveyance shalbe lymyted for the payment of the said yerely rente. And, if the said John the father have no seconde sonne at the tyme of his deathe, or if such seconde sonne be advaunced or preferred as is aforesaid, or after the estate and interest of suche seconde sonne in the last recited mannour and other the premisses in Allerbutler forsayd ended and determyned, then to the use and behouf of the said John Trevillian the sonne, and of the heires males of his bodie lawfully begoten; and, for defaulte of suche issue, to the use and behouff of the said William Trevilian, and of the heires males of his bodie lawfully begoten; and, for defaulte of suche issue, to the use and behouffe of the said Josias Trevilian, and of the heires males of his bodie lawfully begoten; and, for defaulte of such issue, to the use of the heires males of the bodie of the said John Trevilian the father lawfully begoten; and, for defaulte of such issue, to the use of the right heires of the said William Trevilian for ever. And of and in the sayd mannour of Trevilian, withe the appurtenaunces, and of and in all the said messuages, landes, tenementes, and hereditamentes in Trevilian and Sainte Vipe aforsaid, to the use and behowffe of the sayd John Trevilian the father for terme of his lyf, without impechement of waste; and, after his decesse, if the thirde sonne of the said John Trevilian the father lawfully begotten at the tyme of his deathe be not advaunced or preferred by the said John the father to some leasse of landes or tenementes in possession, then to the use and behowffe of the said third sonne until suche tyme as some reversion of landes or tenementes graunted to the said third sonne by the said John the father shall happen to falle, or untill suche tyme as the said John Trevilian the sonne, or the heire male of the bodie of the said John Trevilian the father, shall, by good and sufficient conveaunce and assuraunce in the lawe, assure and convey one yerely rent of tenne poundes of lawfull money of

Englaund, goyng fourth of suche landes and tenementes, wherof he the said John Trevilian the sonne, and the heire male of the bodie of the said John Trevilian the father, shall be seased of a perfecte estate in fee symple without condition or other incombrance: to have and perceave unto the said third sonne of the said John Trevilian the father untill suche tyme as some reversion of landes or tenementes graunted unto the said third sonnè by the said John Trevilian the father shall happen to falle, with one clause of distresse therein to be lymyted and conteyned for nonepayment of the said yerely rente at suche daies and tymes as in the same assuraunce or conveyance shalbe lymyted for the payment of the said yerely rente. And if the said John Trevilian the father have no third sonne at the tyme of his deathe, or if the said thirde sonne be advaunced as is aforsaid, or after the estate and interest of such third sonne of the said John Trevilian the father, the said last recited mannour, and other the premises in Trevilian and Sainte Vipe forsaid, to be ended and determyned, then to the use and behouffe of the said John Trevilian the sonne, and of the heires males of his bodie lawfully begotten; and, for defaulte of such issue, to the use and behowffe of the said William Trevilian and the heires males of his bodie lawfully begoten; and, for defaulte of suche issue, to the use and behowfe of the said John Trevilian and of the heires males of his bodie lawfully begoten; and, for defaulte of suche issue, to the use and behowf of the heires male of the body of the said John Trevylian the father lawfully begoten; and, for defaulte of suche issue, to the use of the right heires of the said William Trevilyan for ever. And of and in the said mannoure of Nettlecombe, Rowden, and Wood Advente, and of and in all the said messuages, landes, tenementes, and hereditaments in Nettlecombe, Rowden, and Wood Advente, with the appurtenaunces (except the capitall messuage and scite of the said mannour of Nettlecombe and the bartons, wastes, milles, and woodis of Nettlecombe and Rowden aforesaid; and except suche messuages, landes, meadowes, pastures, and woods, as are reputed or taken as parte, portion, or member, of the bartons of Nettlecombe and Rowden, or any of them), to the use and behowff of the said John Trevilian the father for and during the terme of his lyef without impechement of waste; And, after his decesse, that the said Thomas Luttrell, Roger Predeaux, William Harris, and Brice Hill, and the survivor or survivours of them, and his or their beires, shall stand and be seased of and in the said last recited premisses with thappurtenaunces (except before excepted) to their owne uses, for and untill suche tyme as they shall and maie levye, raise, perceave, and take of the rentes, issues, and profites of the same premisses for and towardes the advauncement in mariage of the doughters of the said John Trevylyan the father lawfully begoten, which shalbe unmaryed at the tyme of the decesse of the said John Trevilian the father, suche and somuche money as every of the said laste named doughters severally may have therof, the some of fowre hundred markes of lawfull money of Englaund to be severally payd to every one of the said doughters by the said Thomas Lutterell, Roger Predeaux, William Harrys, and Bryce Hille, or by the survivour or survivours of them, or by his or their heires, at the tymes of their severall marryages or at their ages of foure and twentie yeares. And, after such severall some or somes of foure hundred markes levyed as is aforsayd, then to the use of the said John Trevilian the sonne, and of the beires males of his bodie lawfully begoten; and, for defaulte of suche issue, to the use and behowffe of the said Wittm Trevilyan, and of the beires males of his bodie lawfully begoten; and, for defaulte of suche issue to the use and behowffe of the sayd Josyas, and of theires males of his bodie lawfully begoten; and, for defaulte of suche issue, to the use and behowffe of the heires males of the body of the said John Trevylyan the father lawfully begotten; and, for defaulte of such issue, to the use and behof of the heires of the said Wittm Trevilian for ever. And of and in the said mannors of Venyford, Berinarber, Champernehaies, otherwise called Wolmershayes, and of and in the said mannor of Old Knoll, except so myche of the same as lye and be w[th]in Redhuishe, otherwise called Rodhuishe, Cowbridge, Styntwill

Lynche, Torche Lynche, Dunster, Overholte, Westharewoode, and Tymbercomb, aforsaid; and of and in the said capitall messuage and scite of the said mannor of Nettelcomb, and the bartens, wastes, mylles, and woodes, of Nettelcomb and Rowdon forsaid; and of and in suche messuage, landes, meadowes, pastures, and woodes, as are reputed or taken as parte, percell, or member of the said bartons of Nettelcomb and Rowdon, or any of them, with thappurtenances; and of and in all and singuler the said messuages, howses, landes, tenementes, reversions, services, and hereditamentes, with thappurtenances, wherof no use is before by these presentes lymyted nor appoincted, to the use and behouf of the said John Trevilian the father for terme of his lif, wthout impechment of wast; and, after his decesse, to the use and behouf of the said John Trevilian the sone, and of the heires males of his bodye lawfully begotten; and, for defaute of suche issue, to the use and behouf of the said Wittm Trevilian, and of the heires males of his bodie lawfully begotten; and, for defaute of suche issue, to the use and behouf of the said Josias Trevilian, and of the heires males of his bodye lawfully begotten; and, for defaute of suche issue, to the use and behouf of the heires of the bodie of the said John Trevilian the father lawfully begotten; and, for defaute of suche issue, to the use and behouf of the right heires of the said Wittm Trevilian for ever. Provyded alwaies, that if the said John Trevilian the sonne, at his aige of eightene yeares, happen to be espoused and contracted to any other then to one of the doughters of the said Sir John Chichester, or then refuse to marye suche a one of the doughters of the said Sr John Chichester as by the same Sr John, his heires or executours, shalbe lawfully tendred to the said John the sonne, within foure monethes after he shall accomplishe the said aige of eightene yeares, or if the said John the sonne absent hymself, whereby suche tender cannot convenyently be made, or elles if the said John the sonne happen to die before the said aige of eightene yeares, then, if the said Wittm Trevilian at his aige of xviij yeares happen to be espoused or con- tracted to any other then to one of the doughters of the said Sr John

Chechester, or then refuse to mary suche one of the doughters of the said Sr John, as by the said Sr John, his heires, or executours, shalbe lawfully tendred to the same Wittm Trevilian within foure monethes after he shall accomplishe the said aige of xviij yeares; or, if the same Wittm do absent hymself, wherby suche tender cannot convenyently be made, or elles if bothe the said John Trevilian the sonne, and Wittm Trevilian, happen to die before theire aige of eightene yeares, then, if one Josias Trevilian, son unto the said John Trevilian the father, at his aige of eightene yeares happen to be espoused or contracted to any other then to one of the doughters of the said Sr John Chechester, or then refuse to marye suche a one of the doughters of the said Sr John as by the same Sr John, his heires or executours, shalbe lawfully tendred unto the said Josias within foure monethes after he shall accomplishe the said aige of xviijten yeares; or, if the said Josias do absent hymself, wherby suche tender cannot convenyently be made; or elles at such tyme as the said John Trevilian the sonne shall accomplishe the said aige of xviijta yeares the said Sr John Chechester have no doughter in lif and unmaryed above the aige of twelve yeares; or if the said John the sonne happen to die before his said aige, and that at suche tyme as the said Wittm Trevilian shall accomplishe his said aige of xviij yeares the said Sr John Chechester have no doughters in lif and unmaryed above thaige of twelve yeares; or if bothe the said John Trevilian the sonne and Wittm Trevilian happen to die before theire said aige of xviijten yeares, and that at suche tyme as the said Josias shall accomplishe his said aige of xviijten yeares the said Sr John Chechester have no doughter in lif and unmaryed above the aige of twelve yeares, that then and frome thensfourth the said assuraunce and assuraunce to be made as is aforsaid, shalbe, and the said Thomas Lutterell, Roger Predeaux, Wittm Harris, and Brice Hille, and theire heires, shall stande and be seised of and in the said mannor of Whalsborrough, with thappurtenances, and of and in all the said messuages, landes, tenementes, rentes, reversions, services, and hereditamentes, in Whalsborough aforsaid, to thonly use and behouf of

the said Sr John Chechester and of his heires, untill suche ty
the said John Trevilian the father, his heires, executours, or ass
do content and paye or cause to be contented and paide unt
said Sr John Chechester, his executours or assignes, at one whol
entier payment, the some of foure hundreth poundes of l
monye of Englaunde. And, after the said some of foure hun
poundes, paid in manner and fourme aforsaid, the said Tl
Lutterell, Roger Prediaux, Wittm Harris, and Brice Hille, and
heires, shall stande and be seased of and in the said manr
Whalsborrough, and other the premysses with thappurtenen
Whalsborrough forsaid, to thonlie use and behouf of the said
Trevilian the father, and of his heires and assignes for ever
use or uses, thinge or thinges, lymyted or mencioned in these p
Indentures to the contrary in any wise notwthstandinge. Pro
likewise, that, if the said John Trevilian the sone happen to e
or contract hymself to any other then to one of the doughters
said Sr John Chechester, agaynst the will, assent, or consent,
said John Trevilian the father; or if the said John the sonne,
aige of eightene yeares, refuse to marye suche one of the daugh
the said Sr John as shalbe to hym tendred as is aforsaid, or do
hymself in manner and fourme aforsaid; or elles if the said Jol
sonne happen to die before his said aige of eightene yeares, tl
Wittm Trevilian happen to be espoused or contracted or do e
or contract hymself to any other then to one of the doughters
said Sr John, against the wille, assent, or consent, of the said
Trevilian the father; or then if the said Wittm Trevilian at his a
eightene yeares do refuse to marye suche a one of the doughters
said Sr John Chechester as shalbe to hym tendred as is aforsaid,
absent hymself as is aforsaid, or eles if bothe of the said Johr
vilian the sonne and Wittm Trevilian happen to die before thei
aige of eightene yeares, then if the said Josias Trevilian happen
espoused or contracted or do espouse or contract hymself to any
then to one of the doughters of the said Sr John Chechester, a
the will, assent, or consent, of the said John Trevilian the

or then if the said Josyas at his aige of eightene yeares do refuse to
marye suche a one of the doughters of the said Sʳ John Chechester
as shalbe to hym tendred as is aforesaid, or do absent hymself as is
aforesaid, that then and frome thensfourth· the said assuraunce
and assuraunce, so to be made as is aforsaid, shalbe, and the said
Thomas Lutterell, Roger Prediaux, Wiłłm Harris, and Brice Hille,
and theire heires, shall stand and be seised of and in all and singuler
the residewe of the said mannors, messuages, landes, tenemente,
hereditamente, and other the premysses with thappurtenances
(except the said mannor of Whalsborrough forsaid) to the only
use and behouf of the said John Trevilian the father, and of his
beires and assignes for ever; any thinge or thinges herebefore conteyned in these Indentures to the contrary in any wise notwithstandinge. Provided also, and neverthelesse, it is covenaunted, con-
descended, graunted, and agreed, by and betwene the said pties to these
present Indentures, that it shall and maye be lawfull to and for the
said John Trevilian the father, beinge seased of all the said mannors,
messuages, landes, tenementes, and hereditamentes, or of any parte
or percell or member thereof, by meanes, force, or vertu of these
presentes, of any estate of frehold in possession, or elles in reversion,
so that it be not expectant upon any other estate or inheritans, as by
his dede or dedes indented, when and as often as it shall please hym
to demyse, graunte, or lease the said premisses, or any parte, percell, or member thereof, or the reversion or reversions therof, or
any percell therof (except the mansyon houssees and bartons of
Nettelcomb, Rowdon, and Whalsborrough aforesaid, and the landes,
meadowes, pastures, wastes, moores, and woodes, reputed, knowen,
or taken as parte, percell, or member of the said bartones or of any
of them,) to any persone or persones for the terme of one and twentie
yeares, or for any lesser terme or termes, and for no greatter terme
nor termes of yeres, all which terme and termes of one and twentie
yeares or under before mencyoned shalbe accompted to begine at
and frome the makynge of every suche graunte or grauntes, leasse or
leasses, or for the terme or termes of one, twoo, or three lif or lyves

in possession or reversion, jointly or severally by dede indented or by
copye of court rolle accordinge to the coustome of the mannor or
other wise, or for any nombre of yeares determynable upon one,
twoo, or three lyf or lyves in possession or reversion; so that upon
all and every the before named graunte and grauntes, lease and
leasses, so to be made, the olde and accoustomed rent and rentes
or more shalbe reserved and shalbe yearly payable duringe every of
the same graunte and grauntes, lease and leasses, to suche persone
or persones as shall frome tyme to tyme have the imediat reversion
or remaynder therof duringe the same graunte or grauntes, lease
or leasses so to be made as is aforsaid: and so that the said graunt
nor grauntes, lease nor leasses, nor any of them, be made w^th-
out impechement of wast.   And that then and so often the said
assuraunce and assuraunces to be made as is aforsaid shalbe and the
said Thomas Lutterell, Roger Pridiaux, Wittm Harris, and Brice
Hille and their heires, stand and be seised of and in the premysses
(except last before excepted) so to be graunted, demysed, or leassed,
as is aforesaid to the use and uses of suche severall persone and persones, to whome the said premisses or any parte or percell therof
(except last before excepted) shalbe so graunted or leassed, theire
executours, admynystratours, or assignes, for and duringe all
suche and the like terme, termes, and interests as shall be lymyted
upon any suche graunte or grauntes, lease or leasses, so to be made
as is aforsaid, and upon such severall persone and persones to
whome the said p̄mysses, or any parte or percell therof (except last
before excepted) shalbe so graunted or condic̃ons for nonpayment of
the severall rents to be severally reserved upon suche graunts or
leasses, and upon suche other severall condicions, as shalbe lymyted
in the same grauntes or leasses, and annexed to the graunte or lease
of the landes, accordinge to the true intent and meanynge of suche
lease and leasses, graunt or graunts, any thinge or thinges in these
presentes mencyoned or expressed to the contrary in any wise not-
w^thstandinge.   And after the said severall leasses and graunts seve-
rallly ended and determyned, and as the same shall severally end

and determyne, then to suche use and uses, lymytacions, intentes, promyses, and condicions as ben therof before lymyted or appoincted; and to none other use or uses, intents, lymytacions, and provises, any thinge or thinges in these presentes mencyoned to the contrary in any wise not wth standinge. Provided likewise that, if the said John Trevilian the father do at any tyme hereafter demyse or leasse those two meadowes called Cottiford meade and Vellowe meade lyinge within the parrishe of Stokegomer aforsaid, which are reputed or taken as percell of the bertons of Nettelcomb and Rowdon forsaid, or of one of them, or any parte or percell of the said meadowes, or of any of them, to any persone or persones for terme of one and twentie yeares, and do lymyt or appoinct the said terme to beginne and to be accompted at and frome the feast of Easter nowe last past before the date herof, that then the said Thomas Lutterell, Roger Predyaux, Wittm Harris, and Brice Hille, and theire heires shall stand and be seased of and in the said twoo meadowes, or of so muche of the same as shall happen to be leassed as is aforesaid, to the use and uses of suche person or persones to whome the said meadowes or any percell therof shalbe so leassed, theire executours, admynystratours, or assignes, for and duringe the said terme of one and twentie yeares: and, after the said one and twentie yeares ended and determyned, then to suche use and uses, lymytacions, intentes, provises, and condicons, as ben theirin before by these presentes lymyted, and to none other use or uses, intentes, lymytacions, and provyses, any thinge or thinges in these presentes mencyoned to the contrary in any wise not wth standinge. In witnes wherof the said parties to these present Indentures theire seales interchaungeably have set. Yeven the daye and yeare first above wryten.

JOHN CHECHESTER.

Sealled and delyvered in the presens of those persons whose names ar under wretyng.

RYCHARD FORTESCU. ROGER MOLFORD.
ROGER PRYDEAUX. WATER LEY.

CAMD. SOC.

MORTGAGE BY THE MARQUIS OF WINCHESTER TO THE QUEEN.[*]

This Indenture, made the xxiij^th daie of Octobre in the fourtenth yere of the raigne of our most gracious soveraigne ladie Elizabeth, by the grace of God Quene of England, Fraunce, and Ireland, defendour of the faith, &c. Betwene the right honorable Sr John Poulett, knight, Erle of Wilteshire, and Marques of Winchestre, on the one partie, and the right honorable Sr Walter Mildmaie, knight, Chauncelour and Undertresorer of her highnes court of Theschequire, and one of her majesties moste honorable privie counsell; Gilbert Gerrard, Esquire, her majesties Attorney-Generall, and Thomas Bromley, Esquire, her majesties Solicitour-General, for and on the behalf of our said Soveraigne Ladie the Quene, and to the use of her highnes, on the other partie; Witnesseth, that whereas the right honorable William late Marques of Winchestre, and father unto the said now Marques, was indebted and stood bounden to our saied Soveraigne Ladie the Quenes Majestie that now is, by his deed obligatorie bering date the xvij^th daie of June in the tenth yere of her highnes raigne, in the sume of thirtie and fyve thousand poundes, with and upon condition to content and paie or cause to be contented and paied to her highnes, her heires, or successors, at the Receipt of Theschequire, the sume of thirtie-foure thousand one hundred fortie poundes, xv^s 1^d ob. of good and lawfull money of England, at any such daies and tymes as our said Soveraigne Ladie the Quene, her heires or successors, should demaunde or require the same; sithence the making of which bound the said William, late Marques of Winchestre, is departed out of this lif. The saied John, nowe

---

[*] In what way this debt by the late Earl of Wiltshire and Marquis of Winchester had been incurred is nowhere stated, but the sum was large (upwards of 175,000l. of our present money), and Queen Elizabeth was, as we know, very strict in her accounts with debtors. The indorsement on the original parchment-deed is as follows: " A morgage made by the Lo. Marques of divers Mannors unto Sr Thomas (sic) Mildmay, Sr Gilbert Gerrard, and other, to her Matie, for 35,000^li dew to her Matie."

Marques of Winchestre, in consideration and for satisfaction of the sume of foure thousand poundes, parcell of the saied debt of xxxiiij^m cxl^{li} xv^s j^d ob., is contented and agreed to give, graunt, bargaine, sell, and assure, and by these presents doth give, graunt, bargain, and sell, unto the saied Sr Walter Mildmay, knight, Gilbert Gerrard, and Thomas Bromley, all that his newe buildinges, chiefe mancion, or capitall messuage and mannour-house, in Chelsey, in the countie of Midd. with all and singular houses and buildinges, barnes, stables, dovehouses, orchardes, gardaines, landes, tenementes, rentes, and all and singler other the appurtenances whatsoever, which lie or at any tyme were belonging unto the saied nowe Marques of Winchestre, sett, lying, and being in Chelsey aforesaid, in the saied countie of Midd. And also the parsonage of Kingesclere, the graunge of Itchingeswell and Sydmanton, and all the landes and tenementes of the saied nowe Lord Marques in Sherfild-upon-Lodden, with thappurtenances, in the countie of Southt. And also the saied now Marques of Winchestre, in consideration and for satisfaction of other fouer thowsand poundes, parcell of the saied debt of xxxiiij^mcxl^{li} xv^s j^d ob., is contented and agreed to give, graunt, bargaine, and assure, unto the saied Sr Walter Mildmay, knight, Gilbert Gerrard, and Thomas Bromley, the mannors, landes, tenementes, and hereditamentes hereafter in these presentes also expressed: That is to saie, the saied nowe Marques of Winchestre doth give, graunt, bargaine, and sell, by these presentes, unto the said Sr Walter Mildmay, knight, Gilbert Gerrard, and Thomas Bromley, all that the mannour of Hound, with all and singler the appurtenances, in the countie of Southt, the mannour of Townhill-with-Shamelhurste, Boteley, and Mattockesforde, with all and singler thappurtenances, in the saied countie of Southt; the mannor of Nether Wallop, with all and singler thappurtenances, in the saied countie of Southt; the mannour of Abbottes Anne, with all and singler thappurtenances, in the saied countie of Southt; the mannour of Hursborne-Tarraunt, with all and singler thappurtenances, in the saied countie of Southt; the mannour of Turgys, with all and singler thappurtenances, in the saied countie of Southt; three partes of the mannnour of Newneham, with all and singler thappurtenances, in the saied countie of Southt; the mannour of Holshott, with all and singler thappurtenances, in the saied countie of Southt; and all messuages, landes, tenementes, profyttes, commodities, and hereditamentes, estemed, used, reputed, or taken as part, parcell, or member of the saied mannors and other the premisses, or any part or parcell thereof, and the reversion and reversions, remaynder and remaynders, of all and singler the pre-misses, with all and singler their appurtenances; together with all and singler deedes, evidences, and writinges, the premisses before these presentes bargayned and sold, or any and every of them, only concerninge.   To have and to holde all and singler the said mannors, messuages, landes, tenementes, and all and singler the premisses before by these presentes bargayned and sold, with thappurtenances whatsoever, unto the saied Sr Walter Mildmay, knight, Gilbert Gerrard, and Thomas Bromley, their heires and assignes, to the use and behoofe of the saied Sr Walter Mildmay, Gilbert Gerrard, and Thomas Bromley, their heires and assignes, for assurance and suertie of the payment of the saied two seuerall summes of fouer thowsand poundes, parcell of the saied debt of xxxiiij^{m}cxl^{li} xv^s j^d ob., undre the conditions in theise presentes hereafter expressed.   And the saied John nowe Marques of Winchester, for him, his heires, and execu-tours, doth covenaunt and graunt to and with the saied Sr Walter Mildmay, Gilbert Gerrard, and Thomas Bromley, their heires and assignes, by these presentes, that he the same now Marques of Winchestre, the daie of the date hereof, is lawfull and true owner of all and singler the premisses before by these presentes bargayned and sold, and is thereof lawfully seased of a good and perfect estate of inheritaunce in fee simple to his owne use without any condition; and that he hath full power and auctoritie to give, graunt, bargaine, sell, and assure all and singler the premisses in manner and forme aforesaied.   And also that the premisses at all tymes from and after any breach or defaute of payment in these presentes hereafter lymited shalbe discharged, or otherwise from tyme to tyme saved harmles, by the saied Marques of Winchestre, his heires or executors, of and from all former bargaines, sales, gyftes, grauntes, assurances, dowers, recognizances, statutes marchaunt and of the staple, obligations, judgementes, executions, demaundes, and all other charges and incumbraunces whatsoever (other than leasses in possession or reversion, not exceeding the number of fortie yeres from the daie of the date hereof, or three lyves,) and grauntes by coppy of Court-rolle according to the custome of any the saied mannors, and upon which leasses and grauntes the old and accustomed rentes or more byn reserved, and shall and may be yerely unto the saied Sr Walter Mildmay, Gilbert Gerrard, and Thomas Bromley, theire heires and assignes, payable during everie suche interest. And that the premisses in Chelsey aforesaied, in the saied county of Midd. be and for ever hereafter shalbe and contynue of the cleere yerely rent and value of nyneteene poundes, fouerteene shillinges, and three pence, over and above all charges and reprises. And that the saied parsonage of Kingescleere, the saied graunge of Itchingeswell and Sydmaunton, now be, and at all tymes hereafter shall contynue, of the cleere yerely rent and value of xxxvij^{li} viij^s over and above all charges and reprises. And that the saied landes and tenementes in Shirfild-upon-Lodden nowe are, and at all tymes hereafter shalbe and contynue, of the cleere yerely rent and value of xij^{li} x^s viij^d. And that all the residue of the premisses be at this present, and at all tymes hereafter shalbe and contynue, of the cleere yerely value of tow hundred and fyftie poundes over and above all reprises and chardges. Provided alwaies, and it is by these presentes conditioned, and by the said Sr Walter Mildmay, knight, Gilbert Gerrard, and Thomas Bromley, for them and their heires, for and on behalf of our saied Soveraigne Ladie the Quene, her heires and successors, graunted and agreed to and with the saied now Marques of Winchester, his heires and assignes, by these presentes, that, if he the saied now Marques of Winchestre, his heires, executors, administrators, or assignes, or any of them, doe well and truly content and pay, or cause to be contented and paied, to th'use of our saied Soveraigne

Lady the Queenes Majestie, her heires or successors, at the Receite of her Maties Eschequire at Westminster, at, in, or before the feast of the purification of our Lady blessed Mary the Virgyn, next coming after the date hereof, the summe of fouer thowsand poundes of lawfull money of England, in part and towardes the payment of the saied debt of xxxiiij^{m}cxl^{li} xv^{s} j^{d} ob., with out any furder delay, that then and from thence forth aftre suche payment had and made of the saied summe of fowre thowsand poundes as is aforesaied, the gifte, graunt, bargaine, sale, conveyance, and assuraunce, of the saied mannor-house or capitall messuage of Chelsey, and all other landes, tenementes, and hereditamentes whatsoever, with thappurtenances, in Chelsey aforesaied, and also of the saied parsonage of Kingsclere, the grange of Itchingwell and Sydmanton, and of the saied landes and tenementes in Sherfilde-upon-Loddon aforesaid, and of the evidences and writinges concerning the same, by the saied John Marques of Winchester in or by these presentes made unto the saied Sr Walter Mildmay, knight, Gilbert Gerrard, and Thomas Bromley, their heires and assignes, and all and everie use, estate, and interest, by vertue or meanes of the same, shalbe utterly voide and of none effect; and also then and from thence forth it shalbe lawfull unto the saied Marques, his heires and assignes, into all and singler the premisses in Chelsey aforesaied, and in the other places last-mentioned, to re-enter, and the same to repossede, have, and enjoy, to him, his heires, and assignes, for ever, as in his or the former estate. And that then the saied Sr Walter Mildmay, knight, Gilbert Gerrard, and Thomas Bromley, their heires and assignes, and all and everie other person or persons, and their heires, clayminge or that maie clayme in, by, or from them or any of them, shall stand and be seized of such estate as is or shalbe to them conveyed by the saied now Marques or his assignes, of and in all and singler the premisses in Chelsey aforesaid, and in thother places last mentyoned, with their appurtenances, to thonly use and behoof of the saied nowe Marques of Winchester, his heires, and assignes, for ever, absolutely, without any condition, and to none other use or behoofe, any clause, article, or thinge in these Indentures to the contrarie notwithstandinge. And provided also alwaies, and it is by these presentes conditioned, and by the saied Sᵣ Walter Mildmay, knight, Gilbert Gerrard, and Thomas Bromley, for them and their beires, and for and in the behalf of our saied Soveraigne Lady the Quene, her heires and scccessors, graunted and agreed to and with the saied John Marques of Winchester, his beires and assignes, by these presentes, that, if the saied John Marques of Winchester, his heires, executors, administrators, or assignes, or any of them, do well and truly content and paie, or cause to be contented and paied, to thuse of our saied Soveraigne Ladie the Quenes Majestie, her heires or successors, at the Receipte of her highnes Eschequire after the saied feast of the purification of blessed Mary the Virgyn next coming, and at, in, or before the feast of the purification of blessed Mary the Virgyn next ensuinge the date hereof, which shalbe in the yere of our Lord God a thousand fyve hundreth threescore and thirten, the summe of fowre thousand poundes of lawfull money of England, in part and towardes the payment of the saied debt of xxxiiijᵐcxlˡⁱ xvˢ jᵈ ob. without any furdre delay; that then and from thence forth after such payment had and made of the saied last-recyted summe of fowre thowsand poundes as is aforesaied, the gyfte, graunt, bargaine, sale, conveyaunce, and assuraunce, of the saied mannors of Hoyde, Townehill and Shamelhurst, Boteley and Mattockesford, Nether Wallope, Abbotes Anne, Hursborne Tarraunt, Turgys, three partes of the mannor of Newenham, the saied mannor of Holtshotte, and of all messuages, landes, tenementes, and hereditamentes whatsoever, with the appurtenaunces belonging or apperteyning to the saied mannors, and other the premisses last before-mentioned, and of thevidences and writinges concerninge the same, by the saied John Marques of Winchestre in or by these presentes made unto the saied Sir Walter Mildmay, knight, Gilbert Gerrard, and Thomas Bromley, their heires and assignes, and all and everie use, estate, and interest by vertue or meanes of the same, shalbe utterly voied and of none effect. And also then and from thence forth it shalbe lawfull to the saied Marques, his heires and assignes, unto all and singler the saied mannors, and other the premisses last recited, to re-entre, and the same to repossede, have, and enjoye, to him, his heires and assignes, for ever, and in his or their former estate. And that then the saied Sr Walter Mildmay, Gilbert Gerrard, and Thomas Bromley, their heires and assignes, and all and everie other person or persons, and their heires clayminge or that may clayme by or from them, or any of them, shall stand and be seased of such estate as is or shalbe to them conveyed by the saied nowe Marques or his assignes of and in all and singler the saied mannors and all other the premisses last-mentioned, with their appurtenaunces, to thonly use and behoofe of the saied nowe Marques of Winchester, his heires and assignes, for ever absolutely, without any condition, and to none other use or behoofe, any clause, article, or thing in these indentures to the con-trarie in any wise notwithstanding. Provided also, and the saied John Marques of Winchestre, for him, his heires, and assignes, doth covenaunt, graunt, and agree to and with the saied Sr Walter Mild-may, Gilbert Gerrard, and Thomas Bromley, their heires and assignes, on the behalfe of our saied soveraigne Lady, her heires and successors, and it is by the saied Sr Walter Mildmay, Gilbert Ger-rard, and Thomas Bromley, by these presentes graunted and agreed, that if he the same John Marques of Winchester, his heires, exe-cutors, or assignes happen to make defaulte in payment of the saied sum of fowre thousand poundes in these presentes limited to be paied at, in, or before the saied feast of the purification of blessed Mary the Vyrgyn next comying after the date of these present indentures, or of any part thereof, contrarie to the forme before lymited, that then the gifte, graunt, bargaine, sale, conveyaunce, and assuraunce of all and singler the saied mannour and house of Chelsey, and all other the premisses lying and being in Chelsey, Kingescleere, Itch-ingswell, Sydmanton, and Sherfield, aforesaid, shall stand, remayne, and lie to thonly use of our saied soveraigne Lady the Quene, her heires and successors, for ever absolutely without any condition. And he the saied John Marques of Winchester, for him, his heires

score and thirten, or of any part hereof, contrarie to the forme before
lymited, that then the gifte, graunt, bargayne, sale, conveyaunce,
and assuraunce of all and singler the said mannors of Hounde,
Townehill-with-Shamelhurst, Boteley and Mattockesford, Nether
Wallope, Abbottes Anne, Hurstborne, Tarraunt Turgys, three parts
of the mannor of Newneham, the saied mannor of Holshott, and
of all messuages, landes, tenementes, and other hereditamentes
whatsoever, with the appurtenaunces belonging or apperteyning
to the saied mannors and other the premisses last before mentioned,
shall stand, remayne, and be to thonly use of our saied Soveraigne
Lady the Quene, her heires and successors for ever, absolutely,
without any condition.   And also the saied John Marques of Winchester, for him, his heires, and assignes, doth likewise further covenaunt and graunt to and with the saied Sr Walter Mildmay, Gilbert
Gerrard, and Thomas Bromley, and their heires, that if the saied
Marques of Winchester, his heires, executors, administrators, and
assignes, shall happen to make default in payment of the saied
summe of fowre thowsand poundes last recyted, or of any part
thereof, contrarie to the forme aforesaied, that then the said Marques
of Winchester, and his heires, and all other any of them havinge by
or from him the saied nowe Marques (other then such as clayme
only by reason of any the estates or interests before excepted,) at
costes and charges in lawe of our saied Soveraigne Lady, her heires
and successors, shall and will make, doe, and suffer suche further
assuraunce and conveyaunce of all the saied mannors, and other the
premisses, with the appurtenaunces last mentioned in these presentes,
to our saied Soveraigne Lady the Quenes Majestie, her heires or
successors, as by the learned counsell of our saied Soveraigne Lady,
her heires or successors, shalbe also from tyme to tyme reasonably
devised for the better and more suertie of our said Soveraigne Lady,
her heires and successors, in the premisses.   Provided alwaies, and
the said Sr Walter Mildmay, Gilbert Gerrard, and Thomas Bromley,
for them, their heires, and assignes, by these presentes, do covenaunt and graunt, to and with the said Marques, his heires, execu-

tors, and assignes, that from henceforth, untill default shall be made in payment of the saied eight thowsand poundes, or of some part thereof, contrarie to the forme in these presentes before lymited; the saied Marques, his heires and assignes, shall and maie quietly have, hold, and enjoye the rentes, issues, and profits of the saied manñors, lands, tenementes, and hereditamentes, without lett or interruption of the saied Sr Walter Mildmay, Gilbert Gerrard, and Thomas Bromley,. their heires or assignes, or of any other clayming or that shall clayme to have any interest in the same, or any part thereof, by or from them, or any of them, or by the meanes of any of them, which saied rentes, issues, and profits the saied Sr Walter Mildmay, Gilbert Gerrard, and Thomas Bromley, doe by these presentes graunt to the saied nowe Marques, to have and enjoye the same untill default of payment shalbe made contrarie to the forme aforesaied. And the saied now Marques by these present[es] doth covenaunt and graunt to and with the saied Walter Mildmay, Gilbert Gerrard, and Thomas Bromley, that if default shall be made in any of the saied paymentes before lymited, that then within tow monethes next after suche default of payment the saied nowe Marques, his heires or executors, shall pay to th'use of the Quenes Majestie, her heires and successors, at the receit of the saied Court of the Eschequire, the meane rentes, issuez, and profittes of those mannors, landes, tenementes, and hereditamentes, whereof the condition shalbe broken by suche default of payment. In witnes whereof the parties abovesaied to these presentes Indentures interchangeably have sette ther seales. Yeoven the daie and yere first above written.

WA. MILDMAY. (L.S.)

G. GERRARD. (L.S.)

THO. BROMLEY. (No seal.)

CONTROVERSY BETWEEN JOHN AND HUGH TREVELYAN.*

Yt maye please your L.shepp, Touchinge the staye of the *Nisi-prius* betwene they two Trevelians, yf it had bine movid in the tyrme time, yet might have bine grauntted without offence to justice, but nowe after the terme I maye not grant any *supersides* to stay the same, unlese yt had procedid erroniuslie, and sethens I was justice I never grauntted any; and albeit I ame verye lothe to writ to staye procidinges in lawe, yet at your L.shepes motion I have writen a tre to the Justices of Assises ther, so as yt plese your L.shepes and my L. Keper writ also. The justices biginne not ther circut as I hier as yet this xx^th dayes; yt shalbe good the partie travell to them presently to knowe ther myndes therin, and returne ther aunswer to your L.shepe; and yf they will not concent therunto, then I thinke no doubte but upon your L.shepes tres againe thei will procede, acordinge to your L.shepes last mosion in your tre, to have the principall gentellmen of the impannell to pase therin; and so take my leve of your good L.shepe. Cambbridge, this xxiiij^th of July, 1576.

I send to your L.shepe the tre I writt to the Justices herin closed; to that end your L.shepe should perceve the contence therof.

Your L. moste bounden all waye at commandment,

CHRISTOPHER WRAYE.

After my hartye commendacions to you bothe, Her Matie comitted a cause in contreversie betwene the tow Trevelians to my L. Keper and my L. Tresurer and myselfe; my L. Tresurer and I harde the same in Hyllerye terme in the absens of my L. Keper, and in the laste terme my L. Keper, my L. Tresurer and I hard the same

---

* The first of these three official letters (all cotemporary copies) was addressed by Sir C. Wray, Chief Justice of the Court of Queen's Bench, to Lord Burghley, with a copy of the second, " herein closed," to Justices Roger Manwood, puisné judge of the Common Pleas, and John Jeffries, puisné judge of the Queen's Bench ; and the third was written by Lord Burghley to the same two puisné judges. They probably relate to a suit at law, recorded in Plowden's Commentaries, regarding the estate brought into the family by Avice Cockworthy; for an abstract of which see Hodgson's History of Northumberland, Part 2, vol. i. p. 273, note 9 b.

; and, havinge an intention finallye to ende the same, dyd
me wante of confermite in Hughe Trevelian, and yet hopinge
concent ther unto, did forbeare to sertifye her Ma^{tye} of our
nges therin, and so the mater restethe till the next terme,
ge then ether finallye to ende it to ther contentations, or els
ertificatt to her Highnes of our opinions in the same; but we
ideringe the wightines of the cause, the difycultnes did arise
ie hiringe therof, the tediousnes of the matter, and sundrye
had therin, some of one part, and some of another, thought
fitte to be tried at Westminister then in the countrie, wher ye
nall tym for so longe a mater: and declared our opinions to
teis accordingly; wher upon John Trevelyan hathe foreborene
ie anye provision for the same, as he seathe, and Hughe
yan hath taken out an *nysiprius*, mindinge to trie it at the
; for which causes I, thinkinge ye shoulde doe verye well to
lugh to staye, yf he will not abydde our orders as we hoped
lde, yet to staye his *nisiprius*, and take it triable in banke
xt terme, who, havinge warninge therof, nowe taketho noe
eleay or hendrance therby. To this effecte, I thinke, my L.
r will writte to you also, and so bidd you hartylye farewell.
idge, this xxiiijth of Julye, 1576.

Your lovinge Brother,

CHRISTOPHER WRAY. (L. Chief Justice of King's Bench.)

r most hartye commendacions, Wher ther is matter dependinge
reversie betwext the two Trevelians, Hughe and John, which
Majesties exprese order, bothe for the weightines and equitie
cause, hath bine referred unto us two * and to the L. chyfe
to be in equitie heard and ended, wherin we two together
s L. have hade sondrie metinges and conferences, without such
et as we desired, and as we hoppe at some other metinge
er to bringe to passe; notwithstanding, findinge some deffi-

Lord Treasurer (Burghley) and the Lord Keeper (Bacon), as mentioned in the
tter. The latter was evidently expected to have joined in signing this letter,
t does not appear to have done so.

culties which we laboured to ease and remove so well as we might, and partely letted by other busines, that we could not all have comoditye of metinge so as we wolde, beinge now geven to understand that Hughe Trevelian bathe sued out a *nisiprius* and intendethe to have a jurye to trye the causes depending betwext them in contreversie, and by hir M^{ate} for thei causes above specifeed referred unto us, and by us not remittid as yet, as nor intendid to be, for the desier we have by other meane then by processe of lawe to have it endid, and the good causes apearinge unto us that move us ther unto, we have thought good to signifie thus muche unto you by these our letters both of hir M^{ts} good pleasure touchinge these causes, and of our procedinge heretofor and intentions hereafter to proced accordinge therunto, when we shall all three mete againe, yf in the meane tym the trialls do not proced by *nisiprius* befor you, which we think good were forborne for thei causes abovesayde, and for that purpose doe writ these our letters unto you yf you wold in these respects do what you maie to staie such procedinge, lyke as we understande the L. Chiefe Justice hathe to the like effect written his letters also unto you: and hereof we praie you by this bearer to returne us your answers what you intende to doe, for that John Trevelyan, expectinge an end at our handes, is altogether unprovided of councell agenste the Asseses. And so we bied you hartely farewell. Frome the court, this xxvj^{th} of July, 1576.

Your very lovinge frindes,

W. BURGHLEY.

(*To*)
JUSTICE MANWOOD.
JUSTICE GEFFREYS.

MARGERY TREVELYAN'S JOINTURE.*

This Indenture, made the twentithe daye of October, in the sixe and thirteethe yeare of the Raigne of our Soveraigne Ladye Eliza-

* This counterpart is indorsed by John Trevelyan "The counterparte of my wyfes Joynter, Mrs. Margery Trevelyan."

beth, hy the grace of God of Englande, Fraunce, and Irelande
Queene, defender of the faythe, &c. Betwene John Trevelian, of
Nettelcomb, in the countie of Somerset, Esquier, of thone partye,
and John Carter, of St. Columbe Thover, in the countye of Cornewall, gent., and Richarde Kympthorne, *alias* Ley, of Merther, in
in the saide countye of Cornewall, gent., of thother partye. Witnesseth, that the saide John Trevelian, for and in consideration of a
mariadge (bye God his permission) to be hade and solemnised
betwene the saide John Trevelian and Mrs. Margery Blewet, of
Littell Colan, in the saide countye of Cornewall, wedowe, and for a
joincture to be made and assured unto the saide Margery, and for
dyvers other good causes and considerations him hereunto speciallye
movinge, Doth covenaunte, graunte, promise, and agree for him, his
heires, executors, administrators, and assignes, and everye of them,
to and with the saide John Carter and Richarde Kympthorne, and
either of them, their heires and assignes, by these presentes, in manner
and forme followinge, that is to saye, that the saide John Trevelian
shall and will at his owne proper costes and charges, before the feaste
of thappostells Philippe and Jacob nexte ensewinge the date hereof,
knowledge and levye unto the saide John Carter and Richarde
Kympthorne one fyne *sur cognizaunce de droit come ceo qd ils au'ount
de son don* of and in the mannor and lordeshippe of Uthenoe, *alias*
Peryn Uthenoe, with all his appurtenaunces, in the saide countye of
Cornewall, and also of and in all those his messuages, landes, tenementes, houses, edefices, buildings, orchardes, gardens, rentes, reversions, services, knightes fees, courts, perquisites, and profeetes of
courtes, wardes, and marradges, releefes, escheates, wayves, estrayes,
heryotes, amerceamentes, milles, moores, meadowes, pastures, feed-
inges, wastes, commons, and common of pasture, waters, water-
courses, fishinges, poundes, faires, marketes, and hereditamentes
whatsoever, with all and singuler there appurtenaunces, in Uthenoe
Veor, Uthenoe Vean, Trebarveth, Trevean, Nanterant, Golsethnye,
Henforthe, and Trenowe, within the parishe of Peryn Uthenoe, in
the saide countye of Cornewall, and Kenegy, in the parishe of
Breake, neare Helston, in the saide countye of Cornwall. And of

and in all his mesuages, landes, tenementes, rentes, reversions, and services whatsoever reputed, occupyed, allowed or taken as parte, parcell, or member of the saide mannor or tenementes aforesaide, or of everye, anye, or ether of them, into what place or places they or anye of them extende themselves, bye suche name and names as bye the saide John Carter and Richarde Kympthorne, there heires or assignes, or there or anye of there counsell learned in the lawe, shalbe reasonablye advised or devised. Bye which fyne the saide John Trevelian shall knowledge the premisses aforesaide, with thappurtenaunces, to be the righte of the saide John Carter, as those which the saide John Carter and Richarde Kympthorne have in the gifte of the saide John Trevelian. And therebye the same John Trevelian shall release and quit clayme from him and his heires to the saide John Carter and Richarde, and to theires of the saide John Carter for ever. And farther the saide John Trevelian shall bye the same fyne graunte for him and his heires that he the premisses afore-saide to the saide John Carter and Richarde, and to theires of the saide John Carter, agaynste all people shall warrante for ever. Which fyne soe in dewe forme of lawe to be levyed shall be and shall be construed, deamed, and adjudged to be of the premisses, to thonlye uses hereafter in these presentes expressed, lymitted, and declared, and to none other use, intente, or purpose. To weete to the use of the saide John Trevelyan for terme of his lyef, and to the use of all such leases, demises, and grauntes to be made of the said mannor, messuages, landes, tenementes, and all other the saide premisses, with all thappurtenaunces or of anye parte or parcell thereof, by the saide John Trevelian in possession, for .xxj. yeeres or three lyves, or for any number of yeeres determynable uppon 3 lyves. And to the use of all and everve suche person and persons to whome the same or anye parte or parcell thereof shalbe so leased, as aforesaide, uppon which leases, demises, or grauntes thoulde accus-tomed rente shalbe reserved. And after the decesse of the saide John Trevelian, of the reversion and reversions of the saide mannor, mes-suages, landes, tenementes, and all other the premisses, with all the appurtenaunces, and of the rentes, issues, and profeetes thereof (the

patronage and donation of the parishe churches of Mawgan and
Martyn in Meneage, beinge appurtenaunte or appendente to the
saide mannor onlye excepted and foreprised) to the use and behoof
[of] the saide Margery Blewet for and duringe the terme of here
lyef, for and in consideration, name, satisfaction, and full recompence
of all such dower which the saide Margery shall bye the death of
the saide John Trevelian be intituled to have or clayme of anye of
the mannors, landes, tenementes, and hereditamentes whatsoever of
the saide John Trevelian. And after the decesse of the saide Margery of the reversion and reversions of the saide mannor, messuages,
landes, tenementes, and all other the premisses, with all th'appurtenaunces, and of the rentes, issues, and profectes thereof, to the use
and behoof of theires males of the bodye of the said John Trevelian
lawfully begotten or to be begotten. And to the use of all suche
leases to bee made of the saide mannor, messuages, landes, tenementes, and all other the saide premisses, with thappurtenaunces, or
of anye parte or parcell thereof, by anye of the saide heires males
in possession for .xxj. yeeres or three lyves, or for anye number of
yeeres determynable uppon three lyves, and to the use of all and
everye person and persons to whom the same or any parte or parcell
thereof shall be soe leased as aforesaide, uppon which thoulde accus-
tomed rente shall be reserved. And, for defaulte of suche beires males
of the body of the saide John Trevelian lawfully begotten, to the use
of William Trevelian, brother of the saide John Trevelian, and of
theires males of his bodye lawfullye begotten. And, for defaulte of
suche heires males of the bodye of the saide William Trevelian, to the
use and behoof of Josias Trevelian esquier, one other brother of the
saide John Trevelian, and of theires males of his bodye lawfully begotten. And, for defaulte of suche heires males of the bodye of the
saide Josias Trevelian lawfully begotten, to the use of theires of the
bodye of John Trevelian decessed, father of the saide John Trevelian
first named. And, for defaulte of such issue, to the use of the right
heires of the saide William Trevelian for ever. And, ferdermore,

the saide John Trevelian willeth and graunteth that the fyne afor-
saide, in dewe forme of lawe to be leavyed as is aforesaide, shalbe
adjudged, construed, and demed to be for the saide patronage and
donation of the parishe churches of Mawgan and Martyn aforesaide
after the death of the saide John Trevelian, and duringe the lief of
the saide Margery, to thuse of theires males of the bodye of the
saide John Trevelian, lawfully begotten or to be begotten; and, for
defaute of suche issue, to the use of theires of the bodye of the saide
William Trevelian, and of theires males of his bodye lawfully begotten; and, for defaute of such issue, to the use of the saide Josias
Trevelian, and of theires males of his bodye lawfully begotten; and,
in defaulte of such issewe, to the use of theires of the bodye of the
said John Trevelian deceassed; and, for defaulte of suche issewe, to
the use of the right heires of the saide William Trevelian for ever.
And, finallie, the saide John Trevelian doth covenante, promise, and
graunte, for him, his heires, executors, administrators, and assignes,
and everye of them, to and with the saide John Carter and Richard
Kympthorne, their heires and assignes, that the said John Trevelian
shall and will before the feaste of Alsayntes next ensewinge the date
hereof, (for the more better and speedyer assuringe of the saide
jointure to be made and assured to the saide Margery, of and in the
saide premisses in manner and forme aforesaide,) bye his deade of
feoffment sufficient in the lawe, geave and graunte unto the saide
John Carter and Richard Kympthorne, there heires and assignes,
for ever, the saide mannor and all other the saide messuages, landes,
tenementes, and other the premisses with thappurtenaunces; which
feoffement shalbe, and the saide John Carter and Richarde Kympthorne and there heires shall therebye stand and be seased of the
saide mannor, and all other the saide premisses, with all and singuler
there appurtenaunces, to all and singular suche and those same
intentes, and purposes as are here in these presentes before plegraight
layed downe, mencioned, and declared, in manner and forme aforesaide, and to none other use, intente, or purpose, by these presentes.

In Witnesse whereof, the partyes aforesaide to these present Indentures interchangeablye have sette there seales: yeaven the daye and yeare firste above written.

         (L.S.)   (L.S.)

Sigillat' et delib'at' in presentia horum sequent'

    JOHN BLUET, vic.   FRANCYS BLUETT.

   Teste JOHANNE KEMPTHORNE.[a]   WILLM. PEARS.

  Sign. WILLI. + LYELL.   Signum WILL'I + HAWKYNS.

       Signum WILL'I + KEENE.

POPISH EDUCATION OF YOUTH ABROAD.

A coppy of the Counsayles Letters to my Lo. of Bathe.[b]   A.D. 15

After our very hartie comendations. The Quenes majestye fyndynge no small inconvenience to growe unto the realme by sendynge out of the same the children of many gentellmen under colour of lernynge the languages, whereby they ar for the most parte bredde and brought up in the Popysh religyon and corruptness of manners, to the manyfest prejudyce of the state here, which her Majestye, desirous to reforme as a dysorder of no small importance, hath geven order that inquisition be made throughout the realme what sonnes of gentlemen ar at this present beyond the seas, convayed over at any tyme within seven yeres last past, and by what licence they ar gone. And for sych as are departyd out of the realme, yf they be sonnes of any recusants or of sych as do conforme themselves in

[a] John Kempthorne married Eulalia daughter of John Trevelyan.

[b] From a cotemporary copy of the original at Nettlecombe. The document sufficiently explaines itself; and it is to be remembered, with reference to the subject to which the paper relates, that Harington and Dr. Lopez were both executed in this year, the first as a seminary priest, educated in France and Italy, and the second for an attempt on the Queen's life, in order to accomplish the objects of the Roman Catholics in the restoration of their religion. Among the papers preserved at Nettlecombe was the original draft of the Bill of Charges against Dr. Roger Loppes for high treason in 1593, which has been presented by Sir W. C. Trevelyan to the British Museum.

shew only to avoyd the daunger and penalties of the lawes, yt is
not to be doutyd but the intention of ther parentes hath byn to
have them brought up and instructyd in popery, and of thoese many
do become semynarie pryests, Jhesuits, and unsound subjectes, and
sent hether to perverte sych as are dutyfull and well inclined, and to
practice therby to dysturbe the quiett and happy government of her
Majestie. We, therefore, for the better execution of her Majesties
direction in this behalfe, have made speciall choice of you as of persons
in our opynyons meete for your loyallties and affection to her Majestie and the good of the country to be imployed in this service; and
do hereby require and authoryes you and every of you joyntly and
severally by all good meanes to enquire and examyne what gentellmen within that countie have at this present any sonnes, kynsmen,
or other persons, whose education hath byn comytted to ther charge,
or whom they do relyeve or any way mayntayne out of the realme,
being sent over under couler to lerne languages, or for any other
respectes, not beinge notoryusly imployed in her Majesties martyall
services, or trade of marchandyce as apprentices or factors to known
marchantes, and to send us a catalogue of the names as well of the
fathers and parentes, or of ther tutors and patrons, as of the sonnes
and other parties so sent over or mayntayned, in what parties they
ar, and how longe they have byn absent; and of those parentes,
fathers, or other frindes, by whom sych have byn sent out of the
realme; yf any of them be found to be recusantes, or have been evell
affected, and in your knowledge ar but faynedly reformed, you
shall cause bondes to be taken in good sumes of mony to her
Majesties use for ther personall apparance before us by a certayne
day to be by you prefyxed; and, before the bondes so taken, you
shall, by auctorytie hereof, enter and make search within ther houses
for Jhesuites, semynary prestes, and other suspectyd persons, and
apprehend and commytt them to prison, yf any sych shall be found;
as also to open and search in ther closettes, chestes, deskes, and
coffers only for bookes, letters, and wrytings that may any way
conserne matter agaynst the state or the relygion here establyshed,

which you shall seaze and send hether unto us forthwith, sygnifyeng the manner of your prosedynges and your opynions of the men and the matters appearing by your search agaynst them, that we upon ther appearance may take order with them as well for the edvocation of their sonnes or kynsmen, as for any matter that by your indevors may be dyscoveryd agaynst them. And yf the resydence of any of these shall happen to be farr dystant from you, or any one of you, then may you by vertew of these our letters make choyce of some one or tow honest and dyscrete gentellmen, beinge justices of the peace, and not partyally affected towards them, inhabiting nere unto them, to whom you may geve dyrection for the performance of the searche; and for ther pertycular warrant therin you may send unto them a copy of this our letter under your handes, which shall be unto them as suffycient as the originall to you. Herein we requier you to use your best and uttermost indevors with as mytch convenient dylygence as you may to returne us your orderly certyficatt answerynge the severall poyntes of these our letters and dyrections.

So fare you hartely well. From Hamton Courte the last of Desember, 1593.

Your very lovinge fryndes,

Jo. Puckerynge (c.s.)   Wyll. Burghle.

Essex.   C. Howard.

Will. Cobham.   Buckhurst.

Ro. Cecyll.   J. Fortescew.

We leve to your Lordship to appoynt your deputie lieutenantes, and sych of the justyces of the peace for the execution of this service within your chardge, as you shall thynck to be fytt persons for the same.

To our very good lord the Erle of Bathon, Lord Lyeftenant of the Countie of Devon, and in his absence to the Deputie Leuetenantes of that Countie.

THE STATE OF IRELAND.

Advertisement of the xvjth of September, 1595.[a]

595.   The realme is devided into fowre provinces: viz. Ulster, Conocke, Mounster, and Leinster.

Ulster.   The fowrth of this month Sʳ John Norris, L. generall of her Maiesties forces hear, beinge comminge from Armath with her Majesties armye then with him from the victuallinge of the garrisone ther, hee was encountered with the traitor the Earle of Tiron and the northern rebells in that part of Ulster wher the trayterouse Earle lyeth. In which conflict Sʳ John Norris horse was shott in fowre tymes and him self shot in twise with bullet: viz. once in the arm, and thother tyme in the lower part of the bellye glauncinge. The charge was upon the rerereward, where hee, Sʳ Thomas Norris, and all the brave men horse and foot, weare. The traytors toke them upon great advantaige by a wood sied, sufferinge the fore ward and the battell to passe. The generale, percevinge his horse thus hurt to faint under him, and beinge himselfe hurt as afore said, tould his brother Sʳ Thomas Norris, " I have," quoth he, " a ladies hurt. I praie, brother, make this plase good yf you love me, and I will new horse miselfe and retorne presentlie; and I praie charge home." With that Sʳ Thomas, with a brave troup of horse men, one hundred of those that bee under the L. generall, charged, in which charge Sʳ Thomas was shott through the left thiegh, and lost about nyne of his horse men and some few horse in that skirmishe. Wee lost in all about thertye, and the traitors lost ther found dead 60. In thend they fled, and the generall kept the field all night. My cosane Robt. Napp, who is on of Sʳ Thomas prinsipall horse-

---

* Of this document two contemporaneous copies are preserved at Nettlecombe, one of them coupled with a paper of rather a later date. Any information (especially from an eye-witness, such as the writer appears to have been) regarding the state of Ireland at this period, must be interesting.

men, was that daye unhorsed, and he unhorsed the other whom he assalted, and hand to hand he killed his adversarie, and was rescued by one Captaine Gremes, and so horsed agane. He receved a little hurt in one of his armes with a Scottish arrowe. In that part of Ulster where the Earle of Tiron traytorouslie pretendeth domynione, and generalli over all the rest, is the p^t generall with those forces. Neyther Sr John Norris nor Sr Thomas have any daungerous hurt. All this provinst of Ulster is in rebellion, which is more in myne opinyon then the fowrth part of the kingdome. Where the gene-rall lieth ther bee three that taketh on them princli government ther: viz., the traiterous Earle, McQuire, O'donell, and all the rest in that provinst ar adherentes unto them.

Conocke. Towchinge the provinst of Conocke, wherin Sr Richard Bingham is cheef comissioner, which bordereth uppon McQuire and O'donell, a great part of that province have of latt devolted and been in actuall rebellion, as the countie of Sligo, the countye of Letrym, and the countie of Mayo, whereby most of that provinst, is laid wast. The castle of the countie of Sligo, by which the passaige is over a gret water in to Odonell's countrie, was fowre months past taken from Sr Gorge Bingham, and he murdered by some of his Irish sodiers which had secretlie confederated with Odonell, and so kept the same castle for Odonell, by which he maketh incursions into that provinst with great forces. John Martine was taken prisoner ther, but was restored for the brother and mother of the betraier of the castle, and is in health, all though it was advertised unto us that he was slaine. Sr Richard Bingham hathe now supplies from hence of eleven bands of foot and thre hundred horse, bee syeds the ayd of the countrie. Yf hee had not byne ayded from the statt heere, who do resied in the province of Limster, all that provinst had byne lost er this, for thei have bad an exceedinge mislike of Sr Richard. The causes be diversly alleaged.

Sr Richard Bingham hath twise atempted to take the castle againe; but the last tyme he lost 30 men, as it was certified, and hath yet left it. The castle is not of so great importaunce, for ther be dyvers fords in the somer besyeds over the water.

Sr Richard Bingham dothe presentelie set forth a new expedicon, whether into Odonells contrie or not is left to his consideracion. Odonell was in that province of latt, and Sr Richard thought to have intercepted him in his way home ward, but by reasonne he marched daye and night and hasted awaie, and for that our forces came hence but then, and went a longe jornye, and, beinge before wearied, could not march so fast for wearinesse, and so Odonell escaped; other wise I thinke Sr Richard Bingham, uppon those advantages and streaghtes which he might have taken, had utterlie descomfited him, who now standeth allmost as stronge with the ayd of McSwynes, and of certaine Scottes which he hiered, and with the help of the traitors of Conocke, as the traytor the Earle.

This Odonell nor his forces wear with th'Erle all tymes of this conflickt with the L. Generall; but he with all his forces was either then or not to daies before in Conocke, and had a distincte force.

Thus have I left too of our armies, the on attendinge the Lord Generall upon the borders of Tiron against th'Erle the traitor, and thother under the conduct of Sr Richard Bingham in Conocke, which be such forces as I have wrytten, besids the ayd Sr Richard hath of the province. Soe I thinke he ys fifteene hunderd fote stronge, and 400 horse. My countryman Mr. Roberte Williams ys now, the xth of this moneth of September, gon to Sr Richard Bingham—I was muche against yt. God speede him well, hee is a very forward yonge gent. I have assured him hee shall want nothinge.

The province of Monster.—Now, althoughe Sr Thomas Norrice, vice-president of Monster, bee absent, yet that provynce is very quiett.

The province of Lymster.—In this provynce of Lymster, beinge the pale and hart of the realme, the L. Deputye and the state lye. Here was one Fitz McHew, a base fellowe who hath byn theise 30 yeares a great disturber of those parts, whoe dwelled within xxiiij miles of Dublyn. A sharpe prosecucon hath byn made against him, and hee, flyinge still to the woodds and boggs, will never fight, but burne villages and murder, whoe now, by reason of theise warres in the north, uppon his humble peticon wee have taken into mercye uppon proteccon for somme 3 monethes untill her Maiesties pleasure bee knowen.

Because the traytors of Ulster may chuse to fight with which of the Armyes they will, or else may leave both and enter the pale. Therefore my L. Deputy himselfe in person went about seaven dayes past in person to defende the borders of the pale, and hath with him about twelve hunderd foote and 300 horse, and the c. horse which came over with Captayne Dyringe (Deering) doe accompany my L. Deputy.

Before the L. Deputyes departure the domesticall troubles that troubled us nere the cytye were pacifyed.

Account of Expenses, Books, &c.[a]

Layed out for my Master, 1595.[b]

A.D.

Imprimis for a Buckeram bagge	iiij[d]
To the poore people at ij. several tymes . . .	vj[d]
For a quyer of paper	iiij[d]
For half a pownd of pynduste	vj[d]
For thre boockes of Mr. Saclyf's[c]	vij[a]

[a] This account comprises various other items of no interest. Westminster is mentioned, and there is little doubt that all the expenses were incurred in the metropolis. The titles of the books purchased are particularly curious and interesting.

[b] Who " my master " may have been, is not specified, but it was probably some member of the Willoughby family, as, at the back of the slip containing the inventory, if we may so call it, is written, in a different hand, " John Willoughbie his booke," an imitation of the signature of Queen Elizabeth, and several Latin mottoes.

[c] For " Saclyf's " we ought probably to read Sutcliffe's, a controversial divine whose

For peyrce Pennyles [a]	vj^d
For Tarltons Jestes [b] . . . . : . .	vj^d
Delivered to your Wo^p at Westminster . . .	iiij^s
Delivered for your supper at the Horne on Fryday .	iij^s x^d
To Mr. Dr. Smyth for Mr. Williams water [c] . .	xij^d
Robin Goodfelow [d]	vj^d
Hamblett's historie [e]	vj^d
Herball	x^s
Other bookes	xij^s

earliest work, we believe, appeared in 1591, viz. his " Treatise of Ecclesiastical Discipline." Next year he published his " Answer to a certain Libel, &c.;" and, in 1595, the year when this account bears date, his " Answer to Job Throckmorton." These might be the very " three books " mentioned in the account.

[a] " For peyrce Pennyles " can only refer to Thomas Nash's famous tract, " Pierce Penneless his Supplication to the Devil," six times printed in 1592, and often afterwards, on account of its extreme popularity.

[b] " Tarlton's Jests " must have been originally printed soon after the death of that most distinguished actor in 1584, but no edition of the book is known until many years afterwards, viz. in 1611. We may presume that all the earlier copies were destroyed by the thumbs and fingers of careless readers. It was also reprinted in 1630, but the book in any form and of any date is a great rarity. It was reprinted by the Shakespeare Society in 1844.

[c] This item may refer either to the fee paid to Dr. Smyth for giving an opinion upon the contents of a urinal, or it may mean that 12d. were laid out for conveyance upon the Thames—probably the former.

[d] This item must relate to the purchase of an early copy of the well known work, " Robin Goodfellow, his mad Prankes and merry Jests," the first edition of which now known is dated 1628. That it was printed in 1590, or even earlier, can be abundantly proved, and here we see it mentioned in 1595 as having been bought in London. There was, however, a ballad in the form of a chap-book, then also in existence, under the title of " The merry Pranks of Robin Good-fellow, very pleasant and witty."

[e] This is the most valuable entry in the whole of the account, since it proves incontestibly that the old " Historie of Hamblet," upon which Shakespeare founded his tragedy, was in a printed shape in 1595. The only known copy of it bears the date of 1608, five or six years after the play by our great dramatist was brought out. The subject was then unquestionably not new upon the stage, for Nash speaks of a tragedy called " Hamlet " as early as 1587, and we know that in 1594, the year before the date of this account, a " Hamlet " (not Shakespeare's) was acted at Newington Butts theatre.

DEFENCE OF SEATON, BEERE, &c.

A.D. 1596.

the right honourable Wm Earle of Bath, Lorde Leiuetennt
ill of her Highnes Countie of Devon.*

t humblye prayeth your honour to be advertised That whereas
ose names are hereunder written, and the rest of her M^{ts}
subiects of Seaton, Beere, and other parishes nere theirabouts,
ihabite in a place very daungerous by reason that the Bay or
of Seaton aforesaid is such a place, as wherin shippes of a thow-
naie safely ride within musket shott of the shoare, and the same
erie spacious and wyde, and withall verie convenient for ancor-
vherin the enimie of late hath twise sounded and attempted
: enterprises of pill: the same roade beinge on no side garded
lyffs or other defence. In regarde wherof, we your honor's sup-
tes, with some smale healpe of other thinhabitauntes, have
arilie imposed upon ourselves a charge of diverse muskets for
:ter defence of the saide coastinge places. Notwithstandinge,
Honorable, the daungerous premisses not considered, the said
s are appointed to places of service, removed frome the said
and most of the marryners of Seaton and Beere aforesaid de-
for her Highnes service at the sea, and the ordinaunce before
ppointed for the savegard of the said place, by continuance of
nd rust become altogether unserviceable, by which occacions
ntry therabouts ys now become naked of all defence. In consi-
n whereof, and in compassion to the state of the said coun-
, maie please your Honor to geve order that the hundreds of
n, Axminster, Henyocke, Harriage, and Halberton (which

date of this document, 1596, is ascertained from the following indorsement.
Poles and others theire peticions, 24 Aprill, '96·
ordered by the Lo. Leieuetennte and his deputies that the matter herein con-
albe fourthwith ordered by Sr Thomas Denys Knight, one of the Leiuetennts in
sion, and proceedings in that behalfe to be certofied to the Lo. Leiuetennte with
... —W. RAWSON."
are other papers relating to the same matter, appointments of the watch, &c.

by speciall appointment in the raigne of Kinge of Henrie the viij[th] and Queene Marie did contribute towards the maintenance of fower peeces of ordinance, and makinge of bulwarks and other fortificacions their, maie ioyne with the said inhabitants for renewinge of the said defences, or such other defences as by your honor shalbe thought meete. Wherein we hope your Honor shall geve unto us and the rest of her Ma[te] poore subiects their iust cause to besech the Lord to preserve your Lo. with longe lief, with all increase of honor.

JO. WALROND.	ED. WALRONDE.
THOMAS PHILLIPES.	WILL'M STARRE.
JOHN STARR.	NICHOLAS MANSTON.
JOHN MANSTON.	EDWARDE CLARKE.
JOHN PYNE.	JOHN STARRE.
EDMUND STARRE.	ROBART MOXAM.
ALLYNE MARKELL.	ROGER WHIKER.
NICHOLAS HARRIS.	JOHN WILLYAMS.[a]

[a] Among some of the proceedings following this petition for the fortifying of Seaton were "Depositions taken at Colyton before William Pole and John Drake, Esquiers, Justices of Peace, the xxviijth daie of Aprill, 1596."

The depositions are those of six different individuals, and relate to the repairs of the fort at Seaton, and to the hundreds on whom the duty fell of repairing and watching the same. Among them : 4. "John Starr, al. Stere, aiged lxij. yeres or therabout, sworne and examyned, saieth, that, about fiftie yeres last past, he saw the trenches cast at Seeton Marshe; and he likewise sawe one Christofer Cotton make shot of the sea stones for the great ordynaunce there, which ordynaunce were then three quarter-slyngs and two bases.

WM. POLE.
J. DRAKE."

6. "Christofer Cotton of Colyton, aiged fower score and one yere or therabouts, sworne and examyned, saieth,

"That, when King Henry the viij. went to Bullen, (1544) he saw the trench of Seeton marshe new skowred, which was don at the charge of fyve hundreds ; but what those hundreds were he now remembreth not. And further saieth that he was made chefe gunner there and his wages was iiijd. a daye, and could not be paid of that, until Sr John Sentleger, Knight, comaunded Mr. Younge of Axmyster, Mr. Forde of Plymtree, and Mr. Strobridge of Colyton to paie him. At which tyme there were in Seeton three quarter slyngs and two bases.

WM. POLE.
J. DRAKE. " [In

After our most harty commendacions unto you good brethren and Prentyses, trusting in God that you are in good health, as we were at the making hereof. The cause of our wryting unto you at this time is for to know whether you will put up this iniurve or no: for to se our brethren whypt and set on the pyllory without a cause, which is a greyef to us. Desyring you to send an aunswere on waye or other, for yf you will not put it up we do give consent to geather our selves togeather uppon Bartholomew day in the feildes, some with daggers, some with staves, some with one weapon, some with another, such as may be least mistrusted, and to meete in the feyldes betwixt Islington and London betwixt 3 and 4 of the cloke in the afternoone against my Lo. Mayor go to the wrestlinge, and there to be revenged of him; but, yf he go not to the wrestlynge, then to be revenged of him at his house where he dwelleth; and thus we end, comittinge you to God. Amen.

THE EARL OF ESSEX AND TYRONE.

7th of September, 1599.[b]

My Lo. Liftenant Generall of the kingdome of Irelande beinge one   A.D.

In another paper of an earlier date appointing watchers from each of the neighbouring hundreds it is stated, " Provided alwayse, that none shalbe taken to watch except he cometh withe bowe, arrowes, or suffycient armor or weapon."

At a short distance from the village of Seaton is a spot called " Bombshot Green," so named, according to tradition, as a place where stones were chipped into form to be used as shot for the cannon on the Burrow or fort of Seaton, which was on a natural mound of red marle above the beach, but which has since been much reduced by encroachments of the sea.

[a] This paper, only existing, we believe, in a manuscript of the time, from which we copy it, bears date in 1598, and is entitled, " A coppy of a Lybell by the Prentyses of London." It does not appear in our chronicles out of what circumstances it arose.

[b] In his account of the rebellion of the Earl of Tyrone at this period, Moryson (ii. 38)

his marche into the north parte of the realme, whereas my Lo. was mett by tow messengers sente from the Earle Terron. The force of theire messaige was that the Erle Terron woulde ernestly entreate his Lo. to parle with hime, which at the firste my Lo. Generall refused, biddinge hime battaill; but the Earle of Terron desired that, of his honorable favour, his Lop. woulde heąre hime firste speake. They were distante betweene two hilles verie highe, both theire foreces beinge, one under thone side of the one hille, and thother on the other hille, the two hilles were some 2 miles distante asunder; my Lo. generall came rydinge from his forces downe, and the Earle Terron in like sorte, and before he came neare my Lo. generall by 12 scoore paces he was uncovered; and, after he had don his humble dutie to my Lo. generall, he began as foloweth.

" My honorable good Lo., sithe it is not unknowen unto yo.r Lop. howe I married the sister of S.r Henrie Bagnall, and livinge togeather, because I did affecte two other gentellwomen she grewe in dislicke with me, forsooke me, and wente unto her brother to complayne uppon me to the cownsell of Ireland, and did exhibit articles againste me. Uppon this they sente for me; and, because I came not at theire firste sendinge, they proclaymed me trayter, before I never ment to goe out, and so then I had noe other reamedie but goe out to save my heade; and so ever sithence I have beene in this rebellion; and never since hath theire beene, untill the cominge of your Lop. ani debutie that I did dare to put my life into his hands; but, my honorable good Lo., my love to my dreade the Queenes

gives a brief notice of this meeting between him and the Earl of Essex; but he does not relate the conversation, and omits the names of the commissioners appointed to arrange a peace. They are found in the present document, and the whole transaction is related with curious particularity, apparently by a person who was either himself present, or had his information from one who was. The author of "The Lives of the three Earls of Essex," 8vo. 1853 (vol. ii. p. 71,) does not give the same names as members of the commission, and Stowe supplies no information on the subject. The list of the knights slain in battle, or who died in their beds, is also new. Among the captains slain the name of Rich occurs, but this must be a mistake, (unless there were two officers of the name,) for Capt. Barnabe Rich survived his services in Ireland for many years.

Matie, and the love I did beare unto your honorable father deceased, which was such as shall never be put out of my breste. Nexte the love I beare to your moste honorable name and fame in all the worlde, for your prowesse and marshall discipline; holdinge your honer's worde and promise; make me at this time to yealde myself to your Lp. desiringe this to vouchsafe to speake unto the Queene for mercie for me; and by [my] hand I sweare what your Lp. shall thinke fitt for me to doe or undergoe I will, and for ever heareafter wilbe a moste true and loyall subiect, and duringe my life I nor none of my folowers shall holde up hande againste your Lp. excepte it be to save my heade," &c. Unto whose speaches my Lo. Generall answered: " If I were sure you woulde not violate your oathe, and promise as hearetofore you have alreadie don, I would be verie well contente to speake unto the Queenes maiestie, my mistress, for you; and, uppon hope heareof, I will sende my messengers to you with articles, the which, if you will subscribe unto, and sende me in pledges for the performance thereof, I will sende them unto the Queenes Maiestie, and will speake for you to have mercie," &c. The next daie my Lo. sente Sr Gearriet Moore, Sr Edwarde Harbert, Sr William Constable, and Mr. Wotton, one of my Lo. generalles secretories, with othere knights, with the said articles to the Earle of Terron; to the which the Erle of Terron presently subscribed the packett, in the which my Lo. sendinge hearein ar all sente to the Courte, and wee all hope of pease, and that the Earle Terron wilbe a true subiecte (which I pray God graunte), and sende in his pledges.

The names of Knights slayne in Ireland.	S^r Ri. Maistersone.
	Sr Henrie Norris.
	Sr Tho. Norris.
	Sr Conwaies Clifforde.
	Sr Alex^r Ratclife.
	Sr John Sheltton.

Knights which
died in beade. $\Big\{$ Sr Thos Egerton.
Sr Hughe Osburne.
Sr Edwarde Essex.

Captaines
slayne. $\Big\{$ Gardiner.
Baxwell.
Carry.
Prett.
Riche.
Lester.
Wardoman.
Coxe.

THE LORD MOUNTJOYE'S LETTER TO THE COUNSAYLE OF DUBLYN.[a]

601.   After our right hartie commendations to your lordship and the reste, wee doubt not but that you have longe since hearde that, firste O'donnell, after him Tyrone, and lastely Tyrrell, with all the forces they could make, are drawne hither to releeve the Spaniardes in Kinsale, and to force us to raise our seige. They have laine before us a good while incamped in a fastnes betweene the campe and Corke; and had gotten a good parte of the Spaniards that landed lately at Castle Haven to joyne with them. Upon Xtmas Even, beinge the 24th of December, in the morning before day, they were by our scouts discovered to be marchinge towards the towne in good order of battle, with the whole force of horse and foot; haveing agreed, as since wee heare, that, about the breake of day,

---

[a] We are not aware that this communication has ever been published. It is from a contemporary copy preserved at Nettlecombe, but where the original is deposited is not stated, but most likely among the archives of the Irish Privy Council. The indorsement is precisely the same as the above title.

Tyrrell with the vantgard, amongst whome were the Spaniards, should put betwene the Earl of Thomond's quarter and the weste forte, where Don John, with all the Spaniards in the toune, had promised to meete them, and goe upon the other campe; and at that instant Tyrone's two other bodies (which were the battle and the reere) should have sett upon this camp, which they thought their nombers greate enough to doe, assureinge themselves they should be able to make shorte worke of yt, and that none of us should have escaped; but so it hath pleased Almighty God, to whome wee wholly ascribe it, that not above 3 or 400 of our horse, and 2,000 of our foot, beinge drawne out to incounter them (for no more wee could well spare, leavinge our campes well guarded), made them retreat; whome wee followed about two miles from our campe, and in the end charged them verie resoluteley upon a forde where they made a stand with there whole force, and gave them presently an overthrowe, makinge theire horse and foote to run away, being not lesse then 5,000, and the killing, as wee judged, of about 1,200 of them, and the taking of ix. of the cullors where the Spaniards were, who were moste ether slaine or taken; and, since it is affirmed by one that came from them, that themselves account they loste 1,000 men, and had 7 or 800 hurte, besides the losse of there armes, which could not be lesse then 2,000; and had not the wether bene extreeme foule, and our horses weake and not of harte, that wee could no longer followe the execution, being drawne almost two miles from the place where the first charge was given, for so farr wee had followed them, still killinge, wee might have done what more wee could have wished, for they never made any resistance, or looked backe, but were utterly broken. Wee are confident wee shall be no more troubled with those men upon plaine grounde; but that wee may now goe on with our busness for the takeinge of the towne, and hope in God to carrie it within a short time, and have thought fit to signefie so much to you, to whome wee knowe it will be verie wellcome newes, that you may [join] with us in giveing God thankes for so greate a blessinge, and in makinge publique testimony thereof, and impart-

inge it unto such as are well affected, that they may also doe the
like. And so wee bid your Lordship and the reste right hartely
well to fare. From the Campe before Kinsale, the xxvijth of December, 1601.

- - - -- - ---------

COMMISSION FOR COMPOSITIONS.*

After our very harty commendations. Whereas her Matie fynding
her loving subiects much troubled and grieved with sundry warrants and books of concealments graunted in reward for servyce unto
many of her faythfull subiects and servaunts, with a spetyall care of
her highnes part to doe good unto the present tennant in possession.
And forasmuch as shee hath since understood that by some persons
a contrary course hath bene taken, to the great grief and preiudyce
of her people, it hath pleased her Matie to make stay of all such
warrants and books, and now to graunt a commission under the
great seale of England unto us, commaunding us by vertue thereof
to shew all convenyent favour wee may and with speed to dispatche
any her Maties subiects that shall seeke a composition at our hands,
and reformation of any lettres pattents or other graunts wherein
there is any misprision or other defect in the same; And for that
the mannor of Shyrford, parcell of the Pryorye of St. Nicholas in
Exeter, in the county of Devon, was preferred unto us to be rated by
a straunger, upon discoverie of a good tytle which her Matie hath
thereunto; and wee, being infourmed that the same is in your possession, have made stay thereof untyll wee might advertize you,
who by her Maties gratyous meanyng is to have the preferment for

* Original, with autograph signatures. The object, of course, was to remedy the
extortions and other evils connected with the supposed discovery of lands, &c. belonging
to the Crown, the title to which had been fraudulently concealed.

the establishing of your possessyon, yf you doe not wylfully srceasse your tyme; for which purpose wee have appoynted the first daye of the moneth of Maye next ensuyng at Sackevile howse in Flcte Strete, London, to sytt by force of that commyssion, desyring you to come unto us yourself or send some aucthorized from you, who may as there shall be cause come and compound for the same, to her Matie use. And, for redyer dispatche with us, whome her Matie hath appoynted commissioners for such services, wee have appoynted a spetiall person to attend us daylie for such matters, who (being here resydent in London) shall at all tymes be readie to follow this busynes, and acquaynt us with your cause, as occasyon shall serve, yf you shall think so fytt. According to the equytie whereof you may be sure to have a speedie composition, and so be freed from all other troubles. And the arrerages and meane proffitts thereof to be lykewise pardoned, which is one of the chiefest ends of this her Matie most gracyous commission; But, if you shall not attend at the tyme abovesaid, and neclect the benifytt which is intended unto you, Then wee lett you know, that upon your default, wee meane to make composition with such other as have sued for the same. And so wee byd you hartyly farewell. From Sackevile Howse, the first of Aprill, 1601.

Your loving freinds,

T. BUCHURST.

J. FORTESCU.   J. POPHAM.

To our very lovinge Freinde, Mr Rychard Halse, be these dd.

BUILDING OF THE SCHOOLS AT OXFORD.^a   A.D. 1

1613, this 11th of Januarie.

Receaved the day and yeare above written of John Trevillian of Nettlecombe, within the countie of Somsett, Esquier, the sume

^a The first stone of the new foundation was laid 19th July, 1810.

of five powndes of lawfull English monye, beinge his free guifte and bountie towardes the buildinge of the schooles in the Universitie of Oxford., Receaved, I say . . . . . v[ll].

FRAN. JAMES.[a]

---

620. LETTER FROM THE LORD LIEUTENANT OF SOMERSET TO THE SHERIFF,[b] DEPUTY LIEUTENANTS, AND MAGISTRATES, RESPECTING A LOAN TO THE KING OF BOHEMIA.[c]

After my harty commendatons. On Wednesday laste the fourteenth of this moneth I receaved letters from the Rt. Honorable the Lord Ambassador of Bohemia, directed not only to myselfe, but to other the Lords, the Sherife, the Deputy Lieutenants, the Justices of the Peace, the gent[s], and others of the county of Somerset, on the behalfe of the Kinge of Bohemia, touching a loane of money to be had out of the sayd county, which letters I have here enclosed sent you, desiring that you will (for the reasons therein expressed, and for the better manifestation of your zeale, and affections to so good a worke) not only shewe your readines to give good satisfaction herein, but allsoe use your best endeavours to stir up others to doe the like. Thus, not doubting of your performance of the contents of these sayd enclosed letters, I commit you to God, and rest your very loving frende, HERTFORD.

From Lebley this 16th of June, 1620.

To the Right Honorable my very good Lords, and to my very loving Friends the Sheriffe, the Deputye Lieutenants, the Justices of the Peace of the Countie of Somersett.

---

[a] Francis James, of Ch. Ch. Oxon, B.A. 1602, B.D. 1612, D.D. 1614; died in 1621.
[b] Sir John Trevelyan was sheriff of Somerset at this date.
[c] Original; but the subscription only in the autograph of the Earl.

CIRCULAR LETTER FROM THE EMBASSADOR OF THE KING OF
BOHEMIA.

Right Hoble. and my very worthy friends.

I neede not here remonstrate unto you the state of the affaires of
the Kinge of Bohemia my master, for the fame thereof is soe publike
and your affections soe good to the welfare of your soveraignes
children, that you cannot be ignorant thereof; insomuch as I doubt
not but you are partakers of the generall joye and gladnes for those
manifold blessings and prosperities which God hath been pleased .
every daye more and more to conferre uppon them, and will not
exempt yourselves out of the number of those whoe in theire zeale
to the service of the blood royall doe joyntlie contribute to the assistaunce and preservation thereof. The reasons are apparant, and
the meanes offer themselves to our wishes if it please you to laye
hold on them, whereunto I knowe you are well addicted. I have
amongst other thinges receaved chardge from the Kinge my master
to desire the Lord Mayor and his brethren the Aldermen of the
cittie of London, that, in consideracion of the present necessitie of
the affaires of my said master, it would please them to furnishe him
with the loane of a good somme of money. I finde that they are
well disposed that way, yet soe as if they desired to leave a place
open for you and others, the well-affectioned of this Kingdome, to
come in and concurre with them in soe good a worke; and for
example, divers together with those of the cittie have already begun
to enter the lists, namely the clergie and many of the nobilitie and
others, yea some of the principall Lords have made noe difficultie
to embarke themselves therein, and therefore I hope you will not be
the last. That which I soe earnestly entreate is on the behalfe of
the Kinge my master and of his Queene the onely daughter of the
Kinge your soveraigne, the most glorious mother and fruitfull
nursery of the royall plants, the onely consideration whereof and of
those heavenly blessinges which doe soe clearely appeare in her will
incyte you to this holy enterprise, and on the contrary I assure my-

selfe the adverse practizes, apprehensions, or suggestions of others will noe waiea hinder you, especially when the examples of soe remarkable persons of the kingdome as aforesaid, and the examples of some of the shires, doe already leade and encourage you, as alsoe the entire affection of His Matie himselfe, whereof there can be noe doubt made, it beinge unlikely that His Matie will not hartely desire and consent to that which is for the good of his blood and issue. I cannott therefore but hope well of the reall effects of this overture unto you, beinge for the assistaunce and consolation of those whom I assure myselfe you would not wittingly frustrate of the hope and expectation nor of the good opinion which they have of your affections; but that you will rather oblige them by your present and worthy resolutions herein, whereof I promise you a gratefull acknowledgement hereafter under the hands both of the Kinge and Queene of Bohemia, which shall alsoe assure you of the right employement of your favours in theire occasions. I will entreate you to communicate this to all parts of your countie as you shall judge it most proper for the advauncement of soe good and acceptable a worke. And soe committinge you to the protection of the Almightie, and prayeing Him soe to direct you and blesse your counsailes, that they maye tend to His Glorie and the good of His chosen, I take my leave and remayne ever your very assured to doe you service.

Westminster, this last of May, 1620.

20.

LOAN TO THE KING OF BOHEMIA.*

A Course resolved for gatheringe of the lone to the Kinge of Bohemia at the assizes at Tanton. 4 August.

1. The justices of peace have expressed there lone under there hands which were present, and 'tis agreed that the sheriffe shall send the paper to those that be absent.

* The ambassador's letter bears date 31 May, 1620, but Camden informs us that it was not until the 28th of that month that Spinola "set down with his army in the Palatinate,

2. For proceedinge with the country 'tis thought fitt that the justices of peace in there limites shall make choise of 2 or 3 sufficient men within each hundred to make known the letters of the Embassador and the Lord Lieutenant to the able men within the hundred, and to receave of them there lone, and bring it to the justices of the limit.

3. When the monyes are collected, 'tis thought fitt that the justices of the limites doe returne their own lone and the country's to the sheriffe with as much speed as convenientlye may be done, takinge a note from him what they have delivered to the sheriffe.

4. 'Tis agreed that the deputye-lieutenants shall acquaynt the Ld Lieutenant with our proceedings forthwith, and desire to know his L^{ps} direction for disposinge of the monyes when they shall be gathered.

DRAFT OF LETTER FROM THE SHERIFF (SIR JOHN TREVELYAN) A.D. 1
acknowledging the Receipt of £75 0s. 6d. towards the Loan
for the King of Bohemia.

SIR,—I have received by your servant John Fox for the loane to the King of Bohemia from you for your owne and the rest of the justices of your lymitts loane, the severall somes by yourself and them under their owne hands set downe in a paper remayning in my hands, and for the fower Wester tithings xviij li. iij. s. and for the hundred of Milverton xj. li. xviij. s. x. d. whereof I have received in gold seaven peeces of 22s. wantinge in waight 98 graines, an Eliz. xj. s. 14 graines, another peece of xjs. wanting 16 graines. All which amounteth to xxj. s. iiij. d.; and therefore I cannott acknowledge the receipt of 76 li. 1s. 10d. unles the some be made good. soe that I have received in the whole only 75 li. 6d.

There wanteth in the weight of gold xxj. s. iiij. d., and therfore I say rec. only lxxv. li. vj. d. If you therfore send me another acquitt for the rec^t of lxxv. li. vj. d. I will therunto subscribe.

and had appointed that to be the seat of war." The following memorandum is on the back of the document, " Md. 20 Coppies of the Emb. letter and the Lord Lieutenant's and of the Agreements."

CORNWALL.

25.

Information regarding a search for arms, made in the house of John Trevelyan,[a] Esq[r]., inclosed in a letter from the Deputy Lieutenants of Cornwall to the Earl of Pembrooke, dated from " Liskerd, 12th Dec[r]. 1625."[b]

"John Trevilian, Esq[r]. of St. Cleder: taken from him a drum and two mens armes, a musket, and a corslet. The drum is left in the hands of William Coryton, Esq[r]. one of the Deputy Lieutenants; the musket and the corslet is left in the hands of Christopher Worthyvall, Esq[r]. Captaine of that Companye of w[h] the said Mr. Trevillian is. Other or more armes we have not found in any of the Papists' houses, or any popishly affected, yet there are in o[ur] county we conceave neere two hundred psons whose names we shalbe readdy

---

[a] John Trevelyan, the subject of the following letters and depositions, was son of Peter Trevelyan of Basil, in the parish of St. Cleather, Cornwall, whose grandfather Humfrey was one of the seven sons of John Trevelyan of Nettlecombe and Elizabeth Whalesborough, and brother of George Trevelyan, Chaplain to Henry VIII., some of whose letters appear in the first Part of this collection. He is probably the same Mr. Trevillian, a gentleman of Cornwall, who is mentioned in Whitelock's Memorials, p. 200, Feb. 28, 1645, as having " raised a regiment to join with the Parliament's forces." He married Maria daughter of George Arundell.

The papers are interesting as illustrating the inquisitorial nature of proceedings against Romanists, and more especially perhaps as preserving a letter of the somewhat celebrated Bishop, Joseph Hall.

There was about the same time another Mr. Trevillian, spoken of in the Journal of the House of Commons, iii. 678, 26 October, 1644, as being "a very well-affected gentleman of the county of Devon, who has lost all for his good affection and service to the Parliament;" and it is recommended to the Committee for Sequestrations to provide for him "a house furnished." It was probably this same John Trevelyan who in 1645 afforded a refuge at his house in Devon to Philip Powell, a Roman Catholic priest, who was executed at Tyburn in 1646.—*Vide* Memoirs of Missionary Priests, 1742, Pt. 2, p. 298, where he is mentioned as " his old friend John Tre———, in the parish of Yearcombe, in the county of Devon;" and Oliver's History of the Catholic Religion in the counties of Cornwall, Devon, &c. 1857, p. 386.

This John Trevelyan, of Yarnscombe, in the county of Devon, was second son of Anthony Trevelyan, whose grandfather Thomas was third son of John Trevelyan of Nettlecombe, and of Avice Cockworthy, having succeeded to the estate of Yarnscombe from his mother.

[b] State Paper Office, vol. xi. No. 52.

to certifie yor honnour on the least notice from you, which we have not now done, for that your letters requier it not unless they had bin ~~disarmed~~.

CHA: LAMBERT.   RAYNOLD MOHUN.
BAR: GRENVILE.   W. WREY.
WILLIAM CORYTON.

THE JUSTICES OF CORNWALL TO THE KING.[a] A.D. 16

May it please your most excelent Matie.

As your humble servants weare performinge the service commaunded by your Maties last tres touchinge the lieutenancye, on the 8th of this present October, this encloased was brought us from the Right Reverent father in God, the L. Bishop of Exon (by Sr Richard Buller who recd it but the last night by 9 of the clock,) w^t this encloased note, wch is the testimonie of Mr. Nansogg his Ld^{ps} Chapelaine.

We know it to be a greate presumption and bouldnes in us to addresse our tres to yor sacred Matie. But the presumptious threaten so much daunger to y^r sacred pson, the Church, and Comonw^{lth} of England, that in our weake judgments we held them fitt for noe eye but y^r owne; for the pson, he is a Recusant convict; And the greatest of that faction in the West; He is a cloase reserved man, ~~and weighes~~ his wordes before he lets them fall, soe as we conjecture that theare is much more in his hart then on his toungue ; He is of a bould and active spirritt, and the witnes (beinge the L. Bishop's chappelaine) seemes to be of worth; upon these grounds we ar thus embouldened to comend these passages to yor Royall eye; holdinge it the better pte of o^r dutye to be over-fearefull in this kind, then ~~any way remisse~~.

~~We thinke~~ it o^r duties also to enforme y^r Matie how we purpose to

---

[a] State Paper Office vol. cxviii. No. 35.

pceede heere; Immediately upon the dispatche of these we will (by a warrant speciall) comaund the hye-sheriffe to attach (and in safe custody detayne) the bodye of the sayd John Trevilian, whome after his apprehention we purpose to examine, and continew him in durance till y^r Maties farther pleasure be knowne; we will likewise send warrants for the conventinge of Mr. John Prideaux and his wife, all whose examinacõns shall w^t speede be sent up to y^r Matie, and we will attend y^r Maties Comaunds heere untill we receave farther direction towchinge this busines.

    Soe in all humillitye we remaine,
          ready to serve your
               Matie w^t o^r lives,

JOHN MOHUN.	CHA. LAMBART.
RAYNOLD MOHUN.	RICH. BULLER.

Cornwall, 8°. Octo. 1628.

(*Indorsed*,) For your sacred Matie.

28.

THE BP. OF EXETER (HALL) TO SIR RD. BULLER.

Inclosed in the letter of the Justices of Cornwall to the King.[a]

    To my much honored frend, Sr Richard Bulwer, Knight, at Shillington, these.

S^r, w^t my respective remembrance,

I could not but thus suddenly expresse my zeale for the common safety, and care of your indemnity in an occurrent related to mee (this houre) by my Chaplayne Mr. Nansogg. It should seeme he lately acquainted you with certayne dangerous speeches uttered by no meane recusant in the presence of very able witnesses, importing no lesse then the utter and speedy ruine of this whole State and Church: the particulars whereof I have here inclosed. I hope well that you were so sensible of the perill hereof, that you have already

<hr>

[a] State Paper Office, vol. CXVIII. No. 35. Joseph Hall became Bishop of Exeter, 1627, and of Norwich in 1641.

seized upon the party, one Mr. Trevillian, and diligently examined the matter unto the bottom ; as knowing how unsafe it is for any commissioner for the peace to sleep under the notice of so seditious language; if not, let me advise you without all delay to do it, *cum effectu.* The gentleman is knowne to be such as that, if there were not some great confidence in him of the issue, he neither would nor durst let fall such speeches; the sifting whereof may be the prevention of more mischiefe then we can apprehend. Contenting my selfe to have layd this earnest charge upon you (since my selfe am not as yet in the commission, at least not sworne in it), I take my leave, and will think long to know the successe of your present and carefull inquisition, who am your much devoted frend,

JOS. EXON.

Exon. Oct. 4°.

If the speeches be justifyed, you know best know what to do. It is not for me to advise you, but I should think you can do no lesse then send to the Counsayle Table about it.

(The inclosure mentioned above, and in the letter of the justices, is the following testimonie of Mr. Nansogg, the bishop's chaplain.)

John Trevillian of St. Cledar, in Cornwall, gent. said in the hearing of M.r John Prideaux of Trefudder and his wife, that they must change or chuse their religion within this moneth, or their throats would bee cutt, or words to this effect.

2. That they (meaninge Protestants) should expect worse daies, and a greater persecution, then they sufferd in Queene Maries, or words to this effect.

3. That Queene Tibb (interpreting himselfe and naminge Queene Elizabethe) was as arrant a whore as ever breath'd, and that shee was kept by Essex, Leicester, and others, or words to the like effect.

4. That our Bible was composed of lies and tales, or words to the like effect.

CORNWALL.

128. The Examination of Ann Prideaux, wyff of John Prideaux of
Trevorder, in the s⁴ countye, Esqʳ, taken before the Right
Hoᵇˡᵉ Charles Lord Lambert, Sʳ John Trelawny, Kᵗ and Bar-
ronet, and Sʳ Richard Buller, Kᵗ, at Bodmyne, the xiᵗʰ of
October, 1628.ᵃ

The said exam̄, being sworne, sayeth, that she heard Mr. John
Trevillyan of St. Cleder, in the countye of Cornwall, Esq., say
(about three weekes sythence) that, being talking about matters of
religion, that, after the reading of a chapiter, they of the Church of
England did sing a Geneva gygg, meaning one of the Psalms, and
that Mr. Trevillyan sayed unto her that Queene Tibb (interpreting
himself and meaning Queene Elizabeth) was as arrant a whore as
ever breathed, and that she was kept by Essex and Leicester, and
others, or words to the like effect; and she further sayeth she heard
the said Trevillyan say that there was knaverye in our Byble; and
she further sayeth she heard, by one Marshe of Padstow, that one
Mr. Burlace of Newlynd tooke the Byble out of the Viccar of Mer-
ryan's hand, one Smalrudge, and spurned at yt with his foote; and
she further sayeth that Mr. Trevillyan tould her that yf it weere
not for Images wee shalbe all atheists. And Mr. Trevillyan tould
her that yf shee were a Papist shee would be a good woman, and hee
did hope she would turne before shee dyed, and yf shee would not
be a Papist, shee should dye before shee was willing, and have but
a monethes warning, or words to that effect.

ANN PRIDEAUX.

ᵃ State Paper Office, vol. CXVIII. No. 56.

The Examynacion of Martyn Nansogg, clerk, taken before John A.D. 1
Lord Mohun, Baron of Okehampton; Charles Lord Lambert;
Sr Reginald Mohun, K^t and Barron^{tt}; and Sir John Trelawny,
K^{nt} and Baronett; at Bodmyn in the said Countye, the 23^d
daie of October, 1628.[a]

Who saieth that on the 28th daie of September laste he was at
Trevorder at Mr Prideaux his house, when Mrs Prideaux, in the
presence of her husband, told this examynant that Mr Trevillyan, of
St. Clether in the said County, told her that they must change or
chuse their religion within this moneth or their throats wquld be
cutt, or words to this effect.

And farther that they (meaning the Protestants) should expect
worse daies and a greater persecution then they suffered in Queene
Marie's tyme, or words to the like effect.

And farther that Queene Tibb (meaninge Queen Elizabeth,) was
as arrant a whore as ever breathed, and that shee was kept by Essex,
Leicester, and others, or words to the like effect.

And farther that our Byble was composed of Lyes and Tales, or
words to the like effect.

And this deponent farther saith that he understoode that M^{ris}
Prideaux heard these words on the 20th daie of September laste.
And farther that M^{ris} Prideaux told him that Mr Trevillyan had
persuaded her to turne Romaine Catholicke.

And farther this deponent saith that when this depen^t heard these
wordes he said to M^{ris} Prideaux, I wonder with what patience you
and your husband could heare these words, but if I had heard these
words I should have cutt his throate; praye let me have some inke
and paper for I will noate downe these words: Nay, said M^{ris}
Prideaux, pray doe not soe, let him alone, he is too lowe, he is
almost sunke in his estate, and you may have authors enough; or
words to the like effect.

MARTIN NANSOG.

[a] State Paper Office, vol. CXIX. No. 23.

23.   The re-examynacion of Mrs Anne Prideaux, taken *ut supra*.

Who saith that Mr Nansogg beinge with this examynant at her husband's house on the 28th daie of September laste, some weare sayinge that the Papists were like to make a greate head if theare should be any stirr or invasion in England; and then this examynant replyed, Theare is Mr Trevillyan, he is a lusty man; if all the Papists weare such men as he, wee had then cause to feare; when he and I meete, wee are up by the eares, he for the Papists and I for the Protestants, or words to this effect.

And farther this examynant saith that she told Mr Nansogg that some Papists (but who they weare this examynant remembreth not,) that said wee should expect worse daies then they suffered in Queene Marie's tyme, and that faggotts should be deere, and that wee should be burnt if wee did not turne.

ANN PRIDEAUX.

---

138.   COMMISSION TO GEORGE TREVELYAN, ESQ.[a]

Whereas the safety of the kingdome and his Ma^{ts} service is much concerned in the carefull choyce of able and sufficient officers to order and regulate the trayned bands of the severall countyes within his Ma^{ts} dominions in the best and most approved way of military discipline. I have therefore out of his Ma^{ts} trust reposed in me on that behalfe, and out of a due consideracion of the good fame and constant report your sufficiency and aptnes for such an imployment hath deservedly gained you, fixed upon, and doe by theis make choyce of and appoint you to be Captayne of that troope of horse in

---

[a] This document is indorsed, " Mr. George Trevillian's Commission for the command of a Troope of Horse." This troop formed part of Sir Charles Berkeley's regiment, which troop had previously been commanded by Capt. Thomas Jerrard, deceased.

Sr Charles Berkeleyes regiment in the county of Sommersett, lately commanded by Capt. Thomas Jerrard, deceased. And I doe further in my owne pray and require, but in his Ma^{ts} name strictly charge and command you, to the uttermost of your power, to see the same well ordered and disciplined, in such sort that upon all occasions itt may be fitt and ready for his Ma^{ts} service. In the execucion whereof you are to proceed accordinge to such instruccions and direccions as from time to time from my Deputy Lieuten^{ts} or the Collonell for the sayd regiment shalbe given unto you. Hereof you may not fayle; and this shall be your warr^{tt}. Court at Whitehall, the 12th of March, 1638.

PEMBROKE MONTGOMERY.

To my very loving freind George Trevillian, Esq. Capt. of a troope of horse in Sr Charles Berkley's regiment in the county of Somersett.

COMMISSION OF CHARLES I. TO GEORGE TREVELYAN, ESQ,[a] A.D. 1 TO RAISE A REGIMENT OF TWELVE HUNDRED FOOT.

CHARLES R.

CHARLES, by the grace of God King of Great Britaine, France, and Ireland, Defender of the Faith, &c. To our trusty and welbe-loved George Trevillian, Esq., greeting. Whereas a great and rebellious army hath beene raysed against Us under the comūnd of Robert Devereux, late Earle of Essex, which army hath not onely severall times endeavoured to take Our life from Us in sett battailes, but the same and other forces raysed by divers trayterous and seditious persons under the name of King and Parliament, and cherished and mayneteyned by the dialoyall and rebellious citty of London and other parts of the kingdome, have comitted all the acts of outrage, robbery, and murther upon our good subiects throughout

---

[a] From the original, on parchment, preserved at Nettlecombe.

the kingdome, and doe still continue the same, and thereby endeavour to effect their damnable designe to destroy Us and Our posterity, and to change the present government both of church and state into anarchy, tyranny, and confusion. For prevention whereof, and for the defence of Our owne royall person and posterity, the true reformed Protestant religion, the lawes of the land, the liberty and propriety of Our subiects, the just priviledges of Parliament, and the defence and security of Our county of Somersett, Wee being enforced to have in readynesse divers foote well armed, and furnished with all things necessary for Our service, to be employed therein as Wee shall direct, Wee, therefore, reposeing especiall trust and confidence in your fidelity, diligence, and dexterity in martiall affaires, doe by these p'sents will and require you, And doe hereby give unto you full power and authority for Us and in Our name, and for Our service, to imprest, rayse, enroll, and reteyne, one regiment of twelve hundred foote so furnished and armed as aforesaid, wheresoever you shall be able within Our said county of Somersett, who will willingly and voluntarily serve Us for Our pay or wages, as you and they on Our behalfe shall agree. And further Wee do give unto you full power and authority as Colonell them to comand, arme, discipline, trayne, and order in warlike manner, and to employ them for the defence and security of that Our county. Willing and comanding all officers and souldiers, which by virtue hereof you shall reteyne, you to obey, and readily to receive and accomplish your directions and comands in all things hereto apperteyning or necessary to be donne, And you yourselfe to observe and follow such orders and directions as from time to time you shall receive from Our selfe, Our Lieutenant Generall of those parts, or other your superior officer or officers. Farther comanding the High Sheriffe of that Our county, all maiors, justices of the peace, comissioners, and all other Our officers, ministers, and loveing subiects of the said county to be ayding and assisting to you hereby and to all such officers and others as you shall appoint for the furthering and advancement of this Our especiall service; for which this shall be to you and them, and every of them, a sufficient warrant. Given under Our Signe Manuall at Our Court at Oxford, this two and twentieth of March, in the nineteenth yeare of Our Reigne, 1643.

By his Maties comaund, EDW. WALKER.

CAPTAIN SWANLEY [*] TO THE GENTRY OF THE COUNTY OF   A.D.
PEMBROOKE.

GENT.

As in duty bound, I have allwayes in all fidellity highly honoured my Kinge, and ever bine a lover of my Country. Now as I stand engaged, God hath called me to be a servant to both. In discharge of the trust imposed, I am come here to desire your sweete compliance as with me in the preservation of the Gosple in its inherent purity, as allsoe the Kinges honour and the Subject's liberty, a worke that every good Christian ought to be active in, both with the tender of life and fortune; for which yee have the obligation of our Saviour to save you harmelesse, who sayth if any man shall hazard either life or fortune, or what is most deare unto him, " for My sake," shall undoubtedly preserve them. And for your countryes security, you have 3 Kingdomes in the body of the Parliament engaged. Now, why stand yee gazinge like the timerous Israelites over the host of the Philistines? Did not a little youth, David by name, slay their champion, and overthrow that idolatrous hoast? And shall a Jesuiticall and a Popish armye, with a Malignant party, as odious in the sight of God as that cursed Philisten, make you dismayd? Noe, be comforted, God and the state hath preserved you a more visible menes of deliverance in sendinge this fleete, consistinge of 12 warlicke shipps, with land forces and store of ammuni-

[*] This letter of Captain Swanley has been printed in Fenton's Pembrokeshire, 1811, Appendix, p. 27, but apparently from a less correct copy than the present (which is cotemporary), and wanting the date and superscription. We are not aware that the answer has appeared in print before, and it certainly appears to be worth preserving.

tion, whereof the major part is not as yet come in, occasioned by fowle weather, but undoubtedly will arrive. And by God's assistance I am confident, that if the Gentry of this Countye will joyne with me in our endeavours, we shall drayne that Malignant route, who seeke to ensnare this great nation under the yoake of the antichristian beast, not only out of this county but consequently out of the dominion of Wales. Wherefore I shall desire the Gentry of this Countrey to give me theire resolution. And if any of them shall not comply, let not such looke for any favour from me, if it shall please God to give us the victory, but what God's enemyes and destroyers of theire countrey deserve. And let not any man's heart be dismayd, for God hath promised to be with His in his preservinge power eaven unto the end of the world; to whose protection I committ you all, and, expectinge your answer, I remayne and rest ever ready to engage my life with you in the defence of this greate worke,

RICH: SWANLEY.

From aboord His Ma^{tye} ship the Leopard, this 25th of January, 1643.

For the Right Worshipful the Knights and Gent. of the County of Pembrooke these be presented.

·

643.   THE ANSWER.

SIR,

To your letter directed to the Knights and Gent. of the County of Pembroke, we returne this answer. For your much magnifyed fidelity to our gracious Soveraigne we should be glad you could produce better testimony then your owne, and cleerer evidence then your spotted Leopard. For ourselves, we conceive our judgments noe lesse undervalued then our consciences, by youre imagininge the least probability we could be deluded by that stale theme, or affrighted by that citty bugbeare Popery. The disguise of religion is too longe worne, and become transparent eaven unto meane intellectualls. We desire to assert the Protestant sincerity in our

lives, and to act what you professe only, beinge no otherwise inte-
ressed in your blacke aspersions (Jesuitical, Malignant, Antichristian),
then by sorrow that you ar as much estranged from equity as
truth. Yet it is our solace that your callumnyes ar not our
crimes, and our wish that you did noe lesse detest the practice then
the name of a jesuite. As for the devinitye of your letter, we cannot
apprehend it without horror, to see sedition varnisht with scripture,
and God blaspheamed with reverence. But your menaces have
wrought in us noe other impression than contempt, and we had
rather expresse our disdayne by the sword then pen. And you may
rest assured, that if you be soe far wantinge in peace and loyalty as
to invade our country, we will not be soe far wantinge in courage
and duty as not to defend it agaynst all hostile attempts under what
sacred maske whatsoever. This is our firme resolution, which we ar
ready to seale with our blood.

NOTE.—The document given on p. 1 of the First Part of these Papers was incomplete in the transcript, the names of the witnesses having been omitted.   They are here supplied from the original, in the possession of Sir W. C. Trevelyan.

✠ Ego Æðelstan Rex Angloӡ hanc meam donationē cum sigillo
　　Scæ crucis imp̄rsi.

✠ Ego Eadmund indolis clito consensi.

✠ Ego Þulfhelm archiep̄s dictavi.

✠ Ego Ælfheah Ep̄s adquievi.

✠ Ego Æðelgar Ep̄s notavi.

✠ Ego Brihtelm Ep̄s fuvi.

✠ Ego Þȳnsige Ep̄s conclusi.

✠ Þulfgar dux.	✠ Þulfhelm mī.
✠ Ælfhere dux.	✠ Ælfheah mī.
✠ Æðelstan dux.	✠ Ædferd mī.
✠ Odda mī.	✠ Þihtgar mī.

———————

ADDITIONAL NOTE on the last document printed in Part I. p. 218:

This Indulgence was evidently published *before* the suppression of monasteries, probably about the time of the accession of Bishop Veysey to the see of Exeter (1519).   Vide Oliver's History of the Cathedral of Exeter, p. 249.

The type, carefully compared with documents in the British Museum, agrees with that of Pynson, who printed in this country from 1493 to 1531.   Jugge may have used the same type, but he printed *after* the suppression, and therefore could not have been the printer of this paper.

ERRATA IN TREVELYAN PAPERS.

[The following Errata have been pointed out to the Council. Many occur in documents which have been printed from transcripts furnished to the Editor.]

PART I.

			for		read	
Page 137	lines	14 and 21	for	accepting	read	accompting
	—	23	—	Habilie	—	Halalie
138	—	last	—	Lumbert	—	Lambert
139	—	14 from bottom	—	Hurlston	—	Hurlton
	—	9 from bottom	—	vj^d	—	viij^d
141	—	13	—	xl^s	—	xlj^s
	—	9 from bottom	—	cciiij^{xx}	—	ccciiij^{xx}
142	—	10	—	xiij^s	—	xiiij^s
143	—	2	—	Englefelde	–	Eglesfelde
—	—	16	—	x^{ls}		x^{li}
—	—	19	—	x^{li}		xv^{s}
—	—	— note^c	—	Constable of the Tower	—	Master of the Ordnance
144		21	–	brudges	—	of Brudges
145	—	5 from bottom	—	xxiiij^{xx}	—	iiij^{xx}
146	—	18	after	servante	add	in rewarde
149	—	22	for	Bray	read	Bury
—	—	28		no sum	—	cxxxiij^{li} vj^s viij^d
151	—	3	after	Campegius	—	xj^o Maii
—	—	5	for	Marcii	—	Maii
—	—	—	—	DCCxxxiij^{li}	—	cccxxxiij.
	—	3 from bottom	—	v^{li}	—	l^{li}
152	—	7	after	spirituall	—	lerned
—	—	5 from bottom	—	bonfyre	—	making
155	—	6	for	xiiij. die	—	xxiij. die
—	—	9	—	xvj^{li}	—	xj^{li}
—	—	3 of note	—	grace indenture	—	grete indenture
156	—	25	—	Haklnye	→	Hakluyt (see p. 166)
157	—	6	—	xiij^s	—	xliij^s
—	—	7 from bottom	—	Baring	—	Basing
—	—	4 from bottom	—	Pyamontes	—	Pyamountes
158	—	5	—	cxiij^{li}	—	cxij^{li}
—	—	10 from bottom	—	xix^o	—	xxix^o
159	—	17		London, Sir	—	London and Sir
161	after line 24		insert	Paymentes in January a^{o}xxj^{mo}		
164	line	2	add	(the sum paid)—	c^{li}	

note. The Vicar of Croydon was Roland Philipps, D.D. Warden of Merton, college, Oxford. See History of Surrey, by Manning and Bray, ii. 551

Page 167	line	6	for	Pent	read	Penne
168	—	7	—	iiij^{xx} crouns	—	iiij^{xxx} crouns
	—	22	—	alowement		
				amonges the	—	alowance amonges other
174	line	4	for	late Marques	read	Lord Marques
—	—	11		John Skynner	—	Robert Skynner
—	—	13	after	Essex	insert	Sussex
175	—	21	for	value	read	rate
176	—	1	—	fierhookes	—	fierforkes
—	—	7	—	xxv^{li} xiij^s viij^d	—	xxv^{li} xiij^s iiij^d
—	—	27	—	rovers	—	rowers
—	—	—	—	lxiv^{li} iiij^s	—	lxiiij^{li} iiij^s
177	—	8	—	viij^{li} v^s viij^d	—	viij^{li} vj^s viij^d
—	—	18	—	followers		felowis
178	line	8	—	warr. towards	—	warr. for and towards
179	—	1	—	Stawer	—	Scarbro (see p. 167)
—	—	4	—	viijth	—	xiijth
194	—	16	—	twentie yerly	—	twentie pounds yerly
—	—	21	—	xxxiv^{li} xv^s	—	xxxiv^{li} v^s
196	—	10		Montro		Montio
—	—	19	after	nil	insert	quia sol. mens. Decembr. a^o
						R. R. H. viij^{vl} xxxviij^s
—	—	24	for	Benno	read	Bruno
200	—	17	—	Venetia	—	Vicentia
201	—	16	—	xl^s	—	iiij^{li}

203 after Paymentes in February, A° Secundo, insert Sonday at Grenewich
—after line 15   insert   Sonday at West^r

PART II.

14	—	3	for	ut supra	read	suprad^{ca}
—	—	10	—	and	—	a
—	—	20	—	xliiij^{li}	—	xliiij^{li}
—	—	22	—	xlvj^s	—	lxvj^s
—	—	25	—	xxxj^s	—	xv^s
—	—	26	—	xxxj^s	—	xv^s
15	—	6	—	xxx^s	—	xxxj^s
—	—	7	—	Cleoment	—	Clelement
—	—	12	—	plantes	—	planter
16	—	19	after	&c.	insert	xx^s
192	—	20	for	longenge	read	logeinge
194	—	8		Aderne	—	Arderne
—	—	16	after	twentie	—	poundes
—	—	18		Wages	—	at Midsomer 1547
—	—	21	for	xxxiv^{li} xv^s	—	xxxiiij^{li} v^s
—	—	25	—	Huie	—	Huic
—	—	29	—	John Sodo	—	John de Sodo
—	—	—	Item, for John Emyngway yeoman (i. e. yeoman apothecary)			
			lv^s vij^d ob.			
		32	for	Ferris	read	Ferres

INDEX OF PERSONS,

PARTS I. AND II.

₊ The references are to the First Volume where not otherwise indicated.

INDEX OF PLACES.

PARTS I. AND II.

INDEX OF PLACES.

WESTMINSTER :
PRINTED BY J. B. NICHOLS AND SONS,
25, PARLIAMENT STREET.

REPORT OF THE COUNCIL

OF

THE CAMDEN SOCIETY,

ELECTED 2nd MAY, 1862.

THE Council of the Camden Society, elected on the 2nd May, 1862, regret to announce that during their year of office the Society has lost by death the following Members:—

SAMUEL BELTZ, Esq. F.S.A.
THOMAS BROADWOOD, Esq.
The Right Hon. the EARL of ELLESMERE.
The Right Hon. Sir GEO. CORNEWALL LEWIS, Bart. M.P.
The Right Hon. LORD MONSON, F.S.A.
JOHN W. PARKER, Esq.
EDWARD SWAINE, Esq.
CLEMENT TUDWAY SWANSTON, Esq. Q.C. F.S.A.
EDWARD TAYLOR, Esq. Gresham Professor of Music.
Sir ROBERT THROCKMORTON, Bart.
WILLIAM WHATELEY, Esq. Q.C.

The Council still feel it necessary to urge upon the Members the desirableness of bringing under the notice of their friends the claims of the Camden Society to the support of all lovers of historical knowledge. If the list of Members could be filled up, there never was a time when there was a greater opportunity of making valuable additions to Historical Literature than at the present moment.

The following Works have been added to the List of suggested Publications:—

Vindication of the Government of Queen Elizabeth in the matter of the Execution of Mary Queen of Scots. From a MS. in the possession of Sir THOMAS WINNINGTON, Bart. M.P.

Letters of Charles II. From the Originals in the possession of the Marquess of BRISTOL, President of the Camden Society.

The volumes printed for the past year have been—

I. Lists of Foreign Protestants and Aliens resident in England, 1618—1688. From Returns in the State Paper Office. Edited by W. DURRANT COOPER, Esq. F.S.A.

No work issued from the press for many years past has thrown so much light upon the history of families in the Middle Classes of this country. A glance at the many familiar names contained in its very full Index will sufficiently prove its genealogical importance.

The next publication, which is just ready for delivery to the Members, will be—

II. Wills from Doctors' Commons. Edited by JOHN GOUGH NICHOLS, Esq. F.S.A., and JOHN BRUCE, Esq. F.S.A.

The Council refer with great satisfaction to this volume, as proving the success of the endeavours which they have been making for many years to render the materials for our social history, which are stored up at Doctors' Commons, available for literary purposes.

So long ago as on the 26th March, 1848, the Director and Secretary of this Society had an interview, under the authority of the Council, with the Registrars of the Prerogative Court, with the view of procuring some facilities for editing a volume then in course of preparation by the Society. The Registrars declined to comply with the wishes of the Council, and a Memorial in the nature of an appeal having been addressed to the then Archbishop of Canterbury, Dr. Howley, the Council were informed by his Grace that he had no power to interfere.

Subsequent applications for some slight modifications of the stringent rules which limited the use of the Documents in the Prerogative Court were addressed to the late Archbishop of Canterbury and to the Ecclesiastical Courts Commissioners, but were attended with no better results.

On the institution of the Court of Probate the Council, supported by the Society of Antiquaries, and by many eminent literary persons, renewed their endeavours. Sir Cresswell Cresswell, to whom the application was addressed, admitted the principle that documents which had none but literary uses ought to be accessible to literary inquirers; and, as soon as space could be found, Sir Cresswell made arrangements for permitting literary inquirers to consult all wills previous to the year 1700. He also placed this department of the business of the registry of the Court of Probate under the charge of Mr. Paris, a gentleman to whose courtesy to all applicants, and desire to assist their inquiries, the Council are glad to have an opportunity of bearing willing testimony.

With the view of making generally known the importance of the new source of literary and historical information which has thus been laid open, the Council gladly availed themselves of a proposal to publish a Volume of Wills from Doctors' Commons. In this volume it has been endeavoured to give specimens of the Wills of many classes of persons;— Wills of Members of the Royal Family; Wills of Eminent Prelates and Noblemen; Wills of persons who played important parts during the great

Civil War; Wills of well-known Poets, Painters, and Musicians; Wills of Divines and Philosophers; and, lastly, Wills of some distinguished Ladies.

The volume will be very shortly in the hands of the Members; and the Council trust it will be acceptable not only on account of its own intrinsic merits, but as an evidence and memorial, that, after exertions continued for nearly five-and-twenty years, free access has at length been obtained for literary inquirers to nearly all the Records of the kingdom.

The Society will probably think it right to express by a vote of thanks their sense of the public conduct of Sir Cresswell Cresswell, and to transmit with their vote a copy of the printed volume of Wills. They will also thankfully recognise in like manner the kindness of Lord Chief Justice Erle in giving the Editors the use of a transcript of the Will of John Hampden; and that of Francis Kyffin Lenthall, Esq. for the use of a transcript of the Will of his ancestor, the well-known Speaker.

With the volume of Wills will be delivered to the Members, as a third publication for the present year, a second volume of Trevelyan Papers, edited, from the Muniments of the Trevelyan family, by our late Treasurer John Payne Collier, Esq. This volume brings the selection from these curious papers down to 1643.

In concluding their Report, the Council would refer to the continual proof of the usefulness of the Society which is given in the quotation of its books in all recently published historical works. It is now scarcely possible to take up a new historical publication without observing how much the author's researches have been assisted by this Society. A striking instance of this occurred a year or two ago in Mr. Motley's History of the Netherlands; the same thing is found in Mr. Gardiner's recently published History of England during James I. Several of the publications of the Society have been of material service to him, and are continually referred to with due acknowledgment. Such circumstances constitute a strong encouragement to the Society to perseverance, and will prove to persons who are desirous to study the foundations of our history how necessary it is to consult the publications of the Camden Society.

By order of the Council,

JOHN BRUCE, Director.
WILLIAM J. THOMS, Secretary.

15th April, 1863.

REPORT. OF THE AUDITORS.

WE, the Auditors appointed to audit the Accounts of the Camden S
to the Society, that the Treasurer has exhibited to us an account of the
Expenditure from the 15th of April, 1862, to the 15th of April, 1863,
have examined the said accounts, with the vouchers relating thereto, and
to be correct and satisfactory.

And we further report that the following is an Abstract of the
Expenditure during the period we have mentioned.

RECEIPTS.	£.	s.	d.	EXPENDITURE.
By Balance of last year's account..	46	1	10	Paid for printing 600 copies of the " Lists of F Protestants and Aliens " ....
Received on account of Members whose Subscriptions were in arrear at the last Audit..	35	0	0	Paid for Miscellaneous Printing ...... Paid for Lithographs for the " Promptorium Pa rum " ....
The like on account of Subscriptions due on 1st of May last (1862) ..	292	0	0	Paid for Transcripts and Indexes ....
The like on account of Subscriptions due on 1st of May next	9	0	0	Paid for delivery and transmission of Books, Paper for Wrappers, warehousing expenses, &c.
Received for one Composition paid in lieu of Annual Subscription ..	10	0	0	Paid for binding 500 copies of " Parliamentar bates," " Proceedings in Kent," and " Foreign testants and Aliens " ....
One year's dividend on £1016 3s. 1d. 3 per Cent. Consols, standing in the names of the Trustees of the Society, deducting Income Tax..	29	6	10	Paid for binding small numbers of past years' Boo Paid for Insurance........................ Paid for Advertisements ....
By Sale of the Publications of past years to Members of the Society	39	8	0	Paid for postage, carriage of parcels, and other cash expenses......................
				By Balance.........
	£460	16	8	

And we, the Auditors, further state, that the Treasurer has reporte
over and above the present balance of £281 10s. 11d. there are outstanding
scriptions of Foreign Members, and of Members resident at a distance fr
which the Treasurer sees no reason to doubt will shortly be received.

WILLIA
HENRY

15th April, 1863.

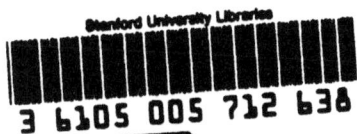

Lightning Source UK Ltd.
Milton Keynes UK
UKOW06f0051190717

305535UK00006B/30/P